Praise for *The Three "Only" Things*

"Robert Moss weaves his three themes of dreams, imagination, and coincidence into an inspiring, insightful, and completely practical way to grow our personal understanding and a transforming vision for others and our collective world. A tour de force by one of the very best practitioners and theorists of contemporary dream and imagework today."

— DR. IAIN R. EDGAR, author of *Guide to Imagework*

"A golden guidebook for waking up the sleeping powers within each person. An essential and energizing read."

— PATRICIA GARFIELD, PHD, author of *Creative Dreaming*

"I would highly recommend *The Three 'Only' Things* to anyone who wants to change the way they think and see the world. Honestly, if there were an instruction book handed out at our birth, it should be this one! It helps us not only to reconnect to our source but to tap into the joy of being that is our soul's purpose."

— DEANNA JOSEPH, BellaOnline.com

"Dream food, coincidence compass, imaginal awakener — Robert Moss has written an erudite exploration that tickles your intellect and at the same time speaks directly to your heart. Read this, and immediately a richer world opens before you."

— JENNIFER LOUDEN, author of *The Life Organizer* and *The Woman's Comfort Book*

"Reading *The Three 'Only' Things* is an exciting journey full of mind-opening information and insight. I had a hard time putting this book down, yet I wanted to so that I could go out in the world of coincidences and tap into the power of my own dreams and imagination with a new perspective. Robert Moss has a gift for reminding us how playful and synchronistic life truly is."

— CHRISTINE HASSLER, life coach and author of *Twenty Something, Twenty Everything*

the
THREE
"ONLY"
THINGS

ALSO BY ROBERT MOSS

Conscious Dreaming
Dreamgates
Dreaming True
Dreamways of the Iroquois
The Dreamer's Book of the Dead

The Way of the Dreamer (DVD)
Dream Gates: A Journey into Active Dreaming (audio)

the
THREE
"ONLY"
THINGS

TAPPING THE POWER OF
DREAMS,
COINCIDENCE
& IMAGINATION

ROBERT MOSS

New World Library
Novato, California

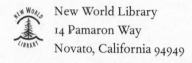 New World Library
14 Pamaron Way
Novato, California 94949

Text design and typography by Tona Pearce Myers

Library of Congress Cataloging-in-Publication Data
Moss, Robert.
   The three "only" things : tapping the power of dreams, coincidence,
and imagination / Robert Moss.
      p.   cm.
Includes bibliographical references and index.
ISBN-13: 978-1-57731-596-4 (hardcover : alk. paper)
ISBN-10: 1-57731-596-0 (hardcover : alk. paper)
1. Dreams. 2. Imagination. 3. Coincidence. I. Title.
BF1078.M67 2007
154—dc22   2007020955

First printing, October 2007
ISBN-10: 1-57731-596-0
ISBN-13: 978-1-57731-596-4
Printed in Canada on 100% postconsumer-waste recycled paper

g New World Library is a proud member of the Green Press Initiative.

10 9 8 7 6 5 4 3 2

*The significant problems we face cannot be solved
at the same level of thinking that created them.*

— ALBERT EINSTEIN

CONTENTS

PART THREE: ONLY IMAGINATION

ON ANOTHER PLANE

How often have you said, "It's only a dream" — to yourself or someone else?

How about, "It's only a coincidence"? Come on, we've *all* said that something is just coincidence.

How often have you told yourself, "It's just my imagination," or, "I'm just making this up"? We routinely dismiss thoughts, feelings, intuitions, and mind-pictures this way, telling ourselves that what we imagine is somehow less than real.

In our everyday speech, in our unconsidered reflexive behaviors, we discount or put down dreams, coincidence, and imagination as *only* this or that.

Ironically, these three "only" things are extraordinary sources of guidance, healing, and power — if we will only pay attention.

Creators, inventors, entrepreneurs, and world changers have always understood this. In this book, we'll learn how Harriet Tubman dreamed the roads to freedom for three hundred escaping slaves; how Wolfgang Pauli, the Nobel Prize–winning pioneer of quantum physics, used dreams throughout his life as his "secret laboratory"; and how Jeff Taylor dreamed up the hugely successful online job agency Monster.com.

We'll find that what has worked for great creators and world transformers is available to all of us. We have the material. We all dream; even the hard-head who says "I don't dream" is only saying, "I don't remember." Whenever we're ready, we can start tapping the nine powers of dreaming.

THE NINE POWERS OF DREAMING

1. *We solve problems in our sleep.*
2. *Dreams coach us for future challenges and opportunities.*
3. *Dreams hold up a magic mirror to our actions and behavior.*
4. *Dreams show us what we need to do to stay well.*
5. *Dreams are a secret laboratory.*
6. *Dreams are a creative studio.*
7. *Dreams help us to mend our divided selves.*
8. *Dreaming is a key to better relationships.*
9. *Dreams recall us to our larger purpose.*

The play of coincidence is all around us, and if we will only *look*, it will teach us that our thoughts and feelings literally generate different events and experiences in the world "out there." We can then begin to work consciously with the law of attraction. We'll see how empires have been governed by the careful monitoring of coincidence, and how serendipity has contributed to many of the most important inventions and scientific discoveries. We'll learn to navigate life and sail into a richer world of possibility by following the nine rules of coincidence.

All of us live by images; they turn us off and turn us on, whether we use our imaginations or are just passive receivers of programming from others. Everything in our lives is different, and charged with magic, when we decide to *choose* the images to which we give our energy and attention and move in the direction of our heart's desires.

We'll learn from masters of the imagination like Leonardo da Vinci, who gave his apprentices a technique for "arousing the mind to various inventions"; Mark Twain, who found universes within the very small; and Joan of Arc and Winston Churchill, who were able to transfer their visions to mobilize whole peoples. We'll find that we can re-make our lives, and our world, by learn-ing and applying the seven open secrets of imagination.

THE NINE RULES OF COINCIDENCE

1. There are things that like to happen together.
2. Thoughts are actions and produce effects.
3. Coincidence multiplies when we are in motion.
4. Life rhymes.
5. The world is a forest of symbols.
6. Every setback offers an opportunity.
7. To find our way, we may need to get lost.
8. Look for the hidden hand.
9. The passions of the soul work magic.

When we claim the power of the Three Only Things, we connect with extraordinary sources of direction, healing, and energy.

We also become citizens of two worlds.

In everyday circumstances, caught up in hurry and stress and other people's schedules and expectations, we often lose touch with the deeper meaning of life. We become entangled in problems that cannot be solved on the level of thinking and being we are on. We are unable to recognize the hidden order of events. We become strangers to magic, which is the art of reaching into a deeper reality and bringing gifts from it into the ordinary world. Worst of all, we forget who we are. We do not know where we come from or where we are going, beyond lists and resumes. We do not remember that our lives may have a deeper purpose and be part of a larger story.

Through dreams, coincidence, and the workings of imagina-tion, we begin to remember that there is a world beyond the obvious one, and that it is there we reawaken to who we are and what we are meant to become. Reawakening to that world is like discovering colors after living in black-and-white. That other world is actually the multidimensional universe within which our 3D reality bobs like a rubber duck in a bathtub. Science knows it is there, and it may be the secret source of all the events that will manifest in the world of the senses.

Through the Three Only Things, we wake up to the secrets of creative living. We become conscious that we are all strange attractors — we attract or repel people, events, and opportunities according to our energy and our state of mind. We come to grasp that there are no impermeable boundaries between inner and outer, subjective and objective. We remember that the passions of the soul work magic, and that our best work is done in the spirit of play. We realize that dreaming is less about sleep than about *waking up*. We learn that the time is always *now* — except when it is *go*.

THE SEVEN OPEN SECRETS OF IMAGINATION

1. By picturing our blocks, we can move beyond them.

2. The body believes in images.

3. If we can see our destination, we are better than halfway there.

4. The Big Story is hunting us.

5. There is a place of imagination, and it is entirely real.

6. We can grow a vision for someone in need of a vision.

7. The stronger the imagination, the less imaginary the results.

All of these things are open secrets. They are knowledge that belongs to us — and can be used by us — as soon as we are ready to reclaim it. As we reawaken to the powers of dreaming, the rules of coincidence, and the uses of imagination, there will be moments when we may be seized with regret that it took us so much time to reclaim tools for living that are profoundly simple, yet have the power to remake our lives and our world.

LIVING BY THE THREE ONLY THINGS

The data in this book is drawn from many sources: from the dream chronicles of the Ottoman court to current scientific research on photon interference, from the ancient I Ching to the Monster.com website, from the correspondence between Winston Churchill and his wife to interviews with entrepreneurs, military leaders, physicians, inventors, artists, and many others for whom the Three Only Things have been a source of success and inspiration. However, the most important data is selected from the thousands of experiences that have been shared with me over the years by people from all walks of life who have attended my workshops, read my books, or been my companions in life adventures.

But, to begin, I want to share some of my personal experiences, because I agree with Mark Twain — an American master of the Three Only Things — when he says, "I don't want to hear about the moon from a man who has not been there."

I've been keeping a journal, on and off, since my teens, and as a dedicated daily practice for more than twenty years. If you are not currently keeping a journal, I hope you'll be inspired to start or restart one by the time you finish this book. When we write in a journal, we make room for a dialogue with the larger Self. We also become alert and alive to recurring themes and symbols in our lives, and gather first-hand data on the play of coincidence and much else.

Because there is so much material in my journals, when I can find a few moments I file the reports in various folders. One of these used to be called "Airline Synch." Now I call it "On Another Plane." The journal entries that go in this folder describe my experiences while catching and traveling on airplanes. Now a plane trip is hardly an exotic event in my life: as a lecturer and teacher, I fly somewhere nearly every week. Whenever I am traveling by plane, I am even more alert than usual to the play of coincidence, especially to chance encounters at the airport or on board the plane. I am extremely watchful when my plans get screwed up, as frequently happens along my flight paths. My local airport is rather small, so flying to most destinations means I need to change planes — often at Chicago's busy O'Hare Airport. Whenever I miss a connection, my antennae start quivering, because I know from experience that when we go off-plan, we enter a liminal area in which a Trickster energy comes into play. In this unexpected territory, very interesting opportunities and encounters may present themselves — if we can forego exhibiting Type A behavior over a delay or an unscheduled event.

I sometimes carry a theme or question with me as I head for another plane. This is one way of playing a game I call Putting Your Question to the World (which I'll discuss in more detail in part 2). In this version, I make it my game to consider anything striking or unusual that happens during the trip as possible guidance on the issue I have on my mind.

At all times, I remain open to the symbolism and serendipity of what is going on within my field of perception. When we operate this way, in a kind of traveling meditation, we let the universe put the questions to us — and a question from the universe can be much more interesting than what is on our personal agendas.

For instance, rushing to make a connection at O'Hare Airport, I once heard a CNN announcer headlining a story about a man who had offered his soul for sale over the Internet. "Soul for Sale" was the phrase that flashed on the TV monitor over the heads of thirsty drinkers at a sports bar. Now *there* was a sobering theme for any life, on any day, and it prompted me to ask this question: "Am I — or is anyone I know — at risk of selling their soul, maybe because we have forgotten we have one?" This led me to think very seriously about a business decision I needed to make and to have a frank discussion with a friend who was worried that his career track was leading him to compromise some of his deepest personal values.

In what follows, I've selected five personal experiences of flight, over a two-year period, from my "On Another Plane" folder. They suggest that we attract or repel people, events, and opportunities according to our energy and our state of mind. They also demonstrate what twentieth-century science has confirmed: there are no impermeable boundaries between inner and outer, subjective and objective. Enjoy!

Bears for the Beloved

April 8, 2005

I am flying to Madison, Wisconsin, to give an evening lecture at Meriter Hospital titled "Honoring the Secret Wishes of the Soul" and to lead a workshop over the weekend titled "Dreaming a Life with Heart."

The man sitting beside me is from Pakistan. Toward the end of the flight, he asks to borrow my pen. He takes two stuffed toys out of a plastic bag. They are both bears. The first is sky-blue. The second, smaller bear is pink and blue and peachy and white.

The Pakistani is filling in little heart-shaped gift cards with my pen.

"Who are the bears for?" I ask him.

"They are for my beloved."

"What is her name?"

"She is called Sabriha. It means 'happy.' But I call her by two nicknames. The first is Arzhu. It means 'desire,' but a *big* desire." He puts his hand on his heart.

"Like the heart's desire."

"Yes, exactly."

"And the second nickname?"

"It's Kuwahish."

"That's a tricky one." I make a couple of attempts to get my tongue around it. "What does Kuwahish mean?"

"It means 'wish,' but a big wish." He sighs.

"Like a wish of the soul."

"That's it."

"In Urdu?"

"How do you know my language?"

"Oh, I've been around."

So — my pen is borrowed to write the words for the heart's desire and the wish of the soul in another language. And I give a lecture that evening titled "Honoring the Secret Wishes of the Soul" and spend the weekend helping people discover and manifest their heart's desires.

Her Dead Mom Got Her the Truck

August 22, 2005

I am crazy-busy the day before boarding my flight to Seattle. On top of everything else I have to do before the trip, my elderly Jeep has made it clear she is on her last gasp, making the sound of a propeller plane as I drive to a dealership; I'm praying she won't die before we get into the lot. Three hours later, thanks to some benign paperwork angel, I drive out of the dealership in a new car, waving farewell to Jeepie.

The last person to get on that Seattle-bound plane claims the seat next to me, breathing hard. I remark that she must have been in quite a rush to make the plane.

"You wouldn't believe it. I managed to buy a new car in two hours this morning and I drove it to the airport parking lot just now."

"That's an interesting coincidence. I was rushing around yesterday buying a new car myself. You beat me by one hour in the transaction time."

"Oh, I couldn't have done it if my mom hadn't helped."

After she catches her breath, she introduces herself. She works in the accounting department of a major insurance company. "Actually, I'm like the internal affairs of our accounting office. I'm the tough lady who looks over everyone's shoulder making sure we don't give free car rental to some poor stiff who's totaled his vehicle if we can avoid it."

Not the most attractive job description, but in person the lady is charming and humorous.

I am intrigued by her mention of her mother as the moving spirit in her car purchase. I have a hunch that Mom is not around in ordinary reality, and I am right.

Ms. Internal Affairs tells me, "My dad's been on his own since Mom passed. Whenever I do something nice for him, Mom does something nice for me. That's how it goes. So I went to see Dad on Sunday, and on the drive back I saw the red truck I have always wanted — the big crew-cabin, four-door Chevy S-10 — right there in a dealer's lot beside the road. I ran in this morning, and everything came together right away. Mom was always a good organizer."

Nothing fuzzy or New Age-y about this lady trucker. She navigates by coincidence without thinking about it, because it gets rubber on the road.

Indiana Jones, Dressed by Churchill's Bodyguard

January 6, 2006

I once dreamed that the poet Yeats — who was a frequent presence in my mind when I was writing *The Dreamer's Book of the Dead* — wanted me to dress in a smarter suit than usual because he was taking me on a visit. When I was correctly dressed, he took me through St. James's Park in London — past the swans — and eventually to Number Ten Downing Street, where he left me to have a private moment with Churchill, who seemed to be engrossed in receiving information on the telephone relating to the magical battle of Britain.

The dream excited and intrigued me. Subsequent research — studded and guided by coincidence — led me to understand that Churchill was deeply interested in the occult and in alternate history. I had always admired Churchill, and I now felt drawn to study him and to write about him. In my imagination, I played with an idea for a fact-based novel with some "Indiana Jones" touches, in which Churchill and his personal network — including one of his bodyguards — would do battle with Nazi occultists, among others.

Now, as is typical, I have another plane trip coming up. Since I have several other book projects on my desk, I resolve to seek a "second opinion" on whether this book plan is really a good one to pursue. I decide that whatever comes up during this trip will be guidance on my theme. To make sure there is no vagueness or confusion about that theme, I write it down on an index card: *I would like guidance on whether writing a novel about Churchill with an Indiana Jones flavor is a good idea.*

On the first leg of my trip, I have an interesting companion, a woman who has recently decided to make radical changes in everything that is central to her life. She has left her husband and her job, sold her home and her furniture. After spending two weeks with a friend, she is now traveling back to an uncertain future. I suggest to her that "if you can *see* your destination, you are better than halfway there."

I ask her to reach down deep inside and tell me what she wants of life.

She begins to talk about an old dream, of founding a center in her hometown that would support women who have been abused or simply defeated by life and help them to find their voice and their power and their healing.

I ask her to *take* me there — to help me see and smell this center, to go there with all of the senses. She warms to this task, and soon we are both *there*, in her dream center. She realizes as she describes the neighborhood that she now has the address — an old building in need of TLC — and that she has identified all the key players, including the financial sponsors, who could make this happen.

When we part company at Chicago's O'Hare Airport, she is juiced and confident.

But she holds my arm for a moment and says, "What do I say to that part of myself that's going to rise up and say, 'It's just your imagination'?"

"You're going to say what the poet Tagore said: 'The stronger the imagination, the less imaginary the results.'"

This is a pleasant exchange (and I like to believe that the center we grew in the imagination now exists). But there is no definite guidance here on my very specific theme, the Churchill novel with an Indiana Jones touch.

Now I am hurrying along the C concourse at O'Hare, dodging snackers and electric carts, heading for my departure gate.

I stop in midstride because at my gate is . . . Indiana Jones.

He has the whole kit: the hat, the jacket, the Sam Browne belt, even the canvas dispatch case. Everything except the whip and the gun.

He does *not* look like Harrison Ford, however. He's considerably chubbier.

And while I am thinking this *may* be my sign, a part of me is also saying: This is absolutely over the top. Just too much. Don't trust this.

So I get on my plane telling myself the verdict is still not in on the theme I have proposed to the universe. I settle down to my in-flight reading, which is a copy of *The Duel*, John Lukacs's masterful study of the personal contest between Churchill and Hitler in the critical months of 1940 when Britain and her commonwealth stood alone against the Nazis. I have just gotten to a page describing Churchill driving with his bodyguard to Number Ten on the day he became Prime Minister when a man looms over me and says, "I'm sitting next to you. I swapped seats with a guy so he could sit with his family across the aisle."

I make room for Indiana Jones, mentally noting that it is always interesting to track what happens when seating plans (or other plans) are scrambled.

"Do you have the whip?" I ask Indiana Jones when he is buckled up.

"It's at home," he explains.

"How about the gun?"

"Got that, too." He knows about guns, he explains. He is in the U.S. Coast Guard, working Homeland Security.

He thumbs his shoulder belt and announces proudly, "You know, this is the real stuff. It was made by Churchill's bodyguard."

"*What* did you just say to me?"

"These clothes were made by Peter Botwright. He used to be Churchill's bodyguard. He went on to make clothes for the actors in the James Bond movies, and then in *Indiana Jones*. I'll give you his website. You can see for yourself."

I show him the open page of my book, where my finger has come to rest on a line describing Churchill in the car with his bodyguard.

"That's quite the coincidence," says Indiana Jones.

"You have no idea."

Yes — I did proceed to work on a novel involving Churchill, one of his bodyguards, and a character with some "Indiana Jones" qualities.

The Bird Plane and the Other Island

October 5, 2006

I am flying to Charlottesville, Virginia, to give a lecture. Before rushing to the airport, I check my email and read a friend's vivid account of watching three immense flocks of Canada geese flying over his house.

I take off in a puddle-jumper en route to Dulles; it's the first leg of my journey to Charlottesville. Ten minutes after takeoff, the plane turns around. We are told we hit "some birds."

When we land, I ask the pilot, "Did we fly into a flock of geese?"

"Yes. Unfortunately, we hit five."

Back at the check-in desk at the airport, there are no seats to be had, for love or money, on alternative flights to Dulles. But a cheerful clerk conjures up the last seat for me on a flight to Charlotte that will connect nicely with a second flight to Charlottesville.

"If I could bet on names," I tell the clerk, "I guess today I would bet on Charlotte."

"Yes, you would." His smile broadens. "My daughter's name is Charlotte, and she just gave birth."

Charlotte-Charlottesville-Charlotte. Some days, we can't help but notice that *life rhymes*.

So now I'm on a different plane, with a different itinerary, and my antennae are twitching. I get goosebumps of confirmation when I see a large black dog at the departure gate. For me, the appearance of a friendly black dog in an unlikely place — like an airport departure lounge — is a very good omen.

As I take off on the "wrong" plane, the attractive woman sitting next to me starts talking to me as soon as she notices the book I am reading: Marc Allen's *The Millionaire Course*. I explain that the book isn't so much about making millions —though they may come with the journey — as about living life to the fullest. I open it at random and read aloud some wise counsel on how people can avoid arguments.

"He could be writing that for *me*," says my neighbor.

We introduce ourselves. She has a movie-star name — Cybille — and she is flying home to an island off the North Carolina coast.

"That sounds like a dream location."

"It's a bad dream. It's the wrong island." She explains that the island is mostly a development for wealthy retirees. Not the place she thought she would be when her husband talked her into buying a home there.

We talk about Marc Allen's approach to growing a vision of an ideal life, and setting the goals and creating the affirmations that help that vision take root in the world.

"I'm a vivid dreamer," Cybille volunteers.

"Do you keep a dream journal?"

"Oh, I always remember my dreams."

"Really? Even after six years?"

"Six years is exactly right. That's when I got married and my dream life changed. Since then, every night I do the same thing — I go to a house on the beach in North Carolina, I spend time with my husband and family, I go to my job. But it's a different house from the one we now own, and a different husband, and a different job. It's like I check out of my present life and go into this other life."

"You're telling me you are living a continuous life, in your dreams."

She nods. "I've never told anyone this before. I know both of my lives are completely real. And I think both of them are taking place in the physical world. Am I crazy?"

"I don't think so. Science is telling us about the probability of parallel worlds. It seems entirely likely to me that when we make a wrenching life choice, our world splits. I guess if I were aware that there is another me, leading another life, I would want to think about what could be accomplished if I could bring both parts of myself together. Have you ever thought about bringing your two selves together?"

"Yes. I know that one day my two lives and my two selves *will* come together."

"And what happens then?"

"Oh, it will be catastrophic." The scary word dissolves in an impish grin. "But it will be very *interesting*."

In this episode, the flow of coincidence brought more than a specific message. It brought a marvelous sense of connectedness and of worlds of possibility beyond the veil of ordinary perception. It carried me into what Baudelaire called the "poetic state of health," in which it is impossible not to notice that life rhymes and that we move among patterns of correspondence. This sequence is also an example of a very practical rule for navigating by coincidence: *Every setback offers an opportunity*. Because my first plane collided with a flock of wild geese, I had the wild experience — on the second, unscheduled plane — of hearing a fascinating first-hand account of a life lived in two parallel worlds. It's hard to complain about a missed connection when it opens a deeper connection and the reward is a story as entertaining as this.

Lincoln's Dreams and the Bull Semen Enhancer

November 11, 2006

I once dreamed I was in a space like the Library of Congress, a place devoted to American history. I walked down a wide, gently sloping hall toward a room filled with books and oak file cabinets.

I paused to listen and talk to a group of wise men. As we conversed, the energy forms of dead presidents drew close to them. When the energy form of a dead president fused with that of a speaker, he embodied the knowledge of the dead president as well as his own and became truly wise.

Outside, I found more people gathered on a green as if for a group photograph. Again, energy forms of past elders were superimposed over the faces and bodies of the people in front of me. A face I found singularly ugly — black bearded, hollow cheeked, deeply pitted or pocked — floated over and around one of the men in the group. I was excited to realize that this could be Abraham Lincoln "coming through."

I suspect that Lincoln — and certainly his Spiritualist wife — would have enjoyed this dream. Lincoln believed that all dreams have significance, and that the best people to help us understand dreams are simple people, "children of nature," who simply do a lot of dreaming. My dream of the dead presidents led me to reflect on how, when we give our best to a certain kind of work or study, we may attract the energy and insight of great minds that are working on another level of reality. It is comforting to think that in times of great danger for a nation or for humanity as a whole, we may be able to draw on the wisdom of elders who have gone before us, whose wisdom may now be deeper than before since they are in a position to view our situation from a higher perspective, with knowledge of possible alternative futures far beyond what we can grasp on our own.

My dream of the dead presidents encouraged me to look again at the role of dreams in Lincoln's life and decision making. I learned that after the premature death of his young son Willie, during the Civil War, Lincoln repeatedly dreamed of his son. He had a recurring dream in which he found himself in a boat without oars, drifting into the mist, a dream that he associated with possible events on the battlefield. Two weeks before he was murdered in Ford's theatre, Lincoln dreamed he was roaming the White House at night, and was surprised to find the place largely deserted — though all the lights were on — until he came to a room where a body was laid out in state. He asked a guard who was dead in the White House and was told the president had been assassinated.

At the time of the Civil War, there was still a *culture* of dreaming in North America. That's apparent in a legend about General George "Little Mac" McClellan, Lincoln's first army chief, who supposedly had a dream or vision in which George Washington appeared to him and showed him the Rebel positions on a map, enabling him to save the capital. This is almost certainly a piece of pious propaganda (though some writers on dreams have been gulled); the interesting thing about it is that you don't invent a *big* dream for political advantage unless you are in a society that takes dreams very seriously.

The story of dreaming in the Civil War goes deeper. "Dream trackers" — people who could see accurately across time and space — were respected by the military on both sides and were put to use. We could call them nineteenth-century "remote viewers," except that this is an unnecessary anachronism, and the best of the dream trackers seem to have done much better than the Pentagon-trained RV guys.

There is a highly instructive example reported in the Richmond, Virginia, *Daily Dispatch* on November 24, 1863. It involves a Confederate soldier who had the gift of tracking deserters to their hideouts. In this particular incident, the dreamer located a deserter who had been well hidden in a smokehouse and secretly fed by his wife for five weeks. Here is the original report, titled "Hid Away in the Smokehouse":

> One day last week one of Captain Shannon's men fell asleep, and while in this mood "dreamed" where a deserter

could be found. He told his Captain of his dream and he immediately sent a squad of men to the place where the young soldier dreamed he was, and found him. Well, reader, where do you think he was? He was in a hole or cellar, all hid away, and things such as barrels, boxes, &c., piled up over him, in his smoke house. There was a small space left open through which his wife fed him. When taken by the cavalry, he begged them to let him see his children, that he had not seen them in five weeks. This is what we call running the thing in the ground. This is not the only deserter that this same soldier has dreamt of and found. We would here say to the deserters (in the way of parentheses) who are in caves and close places, that you just might as well come along and report, because if this man gets a dream at you he'll find you sure.

In the midst of my research on Lincoln and Civil War dreams, I need to catch a plane to lead another seminar. I choose as my in-flight reading a novel by Connie Willis, *Lincoln's Dreams*. In the novel, a contemporary dreamer finds herself — again and again — inside the mind and situation of a Civil War leader, often in harrowing battlefield situations. Her dreams give her accurate information she cannot know from any obvious source. The novel is thrilling and original, with much historical data on Lincoln's life and command decisions. I have just come to a part describing Lincoln's acromegaly — the condition that caused his feet and ears to grow too big — when a man who looks like a prosperous rancher takes the airplane seat next to me.

He opens a book, and when I glance over I see a picture of Lincoln on the page he has reached. I ask my neighbor what book he is reading. The title is *Lincoln on Leadership*. We are both impressed by the coincidence, especially when we discover that neither of us has ever traveled with a book on Lincoln before, and my neighbor has purchased his book only that morning. The coincidence is even more striking because, like me, he has just come to a page in *his* book describing Lincoln's acromegaly.

We talk about what gives great leaders an edge. My neighbor pulls out a little notebook to share a marvelous quote: "We come into our zone where our passion, skill, and experience come together."

I ask my neighbor what business he is in. He tells me that he is a cattle farmer — as I had guessed — but is also "heavy on science." He explains that he has helped to develop a new product that enhances the potency of bull sperm, and he "gender biases" it so that two-thirds of the calves produced will be heifers. He gives me a technical account of the process, then hands me his business card, on which his job description reads: VICE PRESIDENT, SEMEN PRODUCTION AND TECHNOLOGY.

Later on that trip, I show the card to some Chicago women in my seminar. One of them quips, "There are a lot of guys who would love to show that off in East Chicago bars."

This episode was a fine example of one of the rules of coincidence: *there are things that like to happen together*. It encouraged me to pursue my research into Lincoln's dreams, and the larger role of dreams in history, and gave the side benefit of a good belly laugh along the way.

FIVE MINUTES A DAY
TO DISCOVER THE BIG STORY

As we hear stories from many others about the power of the Three Only Things, we'll discover that dreams, coincidence, and imagination are secret engines in the history of *everything*. This is vital to our understanding of the past and to our ability to navigate present challenges and create a better future.

In part 1 we'll learn about the nine powers of dreaming and

how to tap these powers to lead richer, fuller, healthier lives, starting each day with greater energy and insight. Our dreams are constantly coaching us for challenges and opportunities that lie ahead. We see things in our dreams that later take place in physical reality; this is called precognition. We also see things that may or may not happen, depending on whether we do something with the information. We preview a car accident we may be able to avoid if we use the dream as a travel advisory. We get a glimpse of our ideal job, or the perfect home, or even the partner of our soul — but that wonderful dream may not manifest in the world unless we get the details straight and take appropriate action.

Our dreams start preparing us for what life will give us months, years, even decades into the future. For instance, when he was just fourteen, Winston Churchill told a school friend at Harrow that he had dreamed that one day he would be required to lead the country and "save the capital and the empire."

We'll find that dreamers — so far from being impractical or floaty — are often highly successful in their chosen fields of endeavor because they are able to see far beyond the present horizon and draw energy from their vision. Howard Schultz, the founder of Starbucks, says of himself, "My most marked characteristic is the ability to dream more than most think practical."

In part 2, we'll confirm that coincidence is never "only" anything, and we'll learn how to track coincidences and the symbols of everyday life as homing beacons. A stream of coincidence alerts us to the fact that we are not alone, that we have invisible sources of support, and that we may be on the right course even when the whole world seems to be going the other way — or alternatively, that we may need to adjust our goals and behaviors to a deeper agenda. We'll learn that by working with the nine rules of coincidence, we can use *anything* that enters our field of perception as a personal oracle and charge our everyday lives with creative juice.

In part 3, we'll learn the *practice* of imagination: the fabulous art of "making things up" — and finding they are altogether real. The greatest crisis in our lives is a crisis of imagination. We get stuck and bind ourselves to the wheel of repetition because we refuse to reimagine our situation. We live with a set of negative or confining images and pronounce them "reality."

To live the fullest, juiciest lives, we need to invest our energy and attention in a form of active imagination that dares to re-vision everything. We'll accomplish this by learning and applying the seven open secrets of imagination, including the great truth that Rabindranath Tagore expressed, with poetic insight, when he wrote: "The stronger the imagination, the less imaginary the results."

We'll build a home in the imagination and use it as a place of healing, relaxation, and creative inspiration — and we'll learn how to manifest the best things we grow there in our everyday lives.

In just five minutes a day, we can tap the power of the Three Only Things in fun and practical ways. Each section of the book offers fabulous games we can play in the thick of everyday life. These simple exercises allow us to tap into extraordinary sources and resources that can give us a winning edge, as they have done for many highly creative and successful people.

But paying attention to the Three Only Things gives us much more than a winning edge.

Living this way — even for just five minutes of dedicated time each day — we put ourselves in touch with our inner truth. We find our inner compass and get a "second opinion" on vital personal issues in the midst of confusion and conflicting agendas. We open and sustain a dialogue with a Self that is wiser than what Yeats called "the daily trivial mind."

We allow ourselves to move effortlessly into creative flow.

We also allow our Big Stories to reveal themselves. Australian

Aborigines say Big Stories hunt the right people to tell them, like predators stalking and sniffing in the bush. The trick is not to go chasing them, but to let them catch up with us.

Sometimes a Big Story seizes us through a riff of coincidence we simply cannot dismiss. When we are seized by a Big Story, our lives are different. We have the power to cope with everyday dramas with greater courage and grace, because we are aware of a deeper drama. We have access to *mythic* resources, in the sense Joseph Campbell conveyed when he reminded us that healing is what happens when we "move beyond suffering into myth." We now travel with a sense of mission, and when we travel with that sense of mission, we draw different events and people and opportunities toward us.

We make ourselves available to the Big Stories when we make room in our lives for dreams, coincidence, and the play of imagination.

ONLY a DREAM

God created the dream to show
the way to the dreamer in his blindness.

— PAPYRUS INSINGER, LATE EGYPTIAN DEMOTIC WISDOM TEXT

DREAMING IS WAKING UP

L et's try it again: How often have you said, "It's only a dream"? You may have said this to yourself when you wanted to forget about something that troubled you during the night, wishing that issue away.

Maybe you said it wistfully, surfacing from a dream in which you were enjoying beauty and pleasure that seemed unattainable in ordinary life.

As we rush or stumble into the business of the day, it's easy for us to leave our dreams behind. A door slams shut in the mind, and the dreams are gone. It's poor strategy in life to let that happen. Here's why:

Dreams are not on our case, they are on our side.

They open vistas of possibility that take us beyond our everyday self-limiting beliefs and behaviors. Before we dismiss our dream lover, our dream home, or our dream job as unattainable — "only a dream" — we want to examine carefully whether there are clues in the dream that could help us to manifest that juicy vision.

Our dreams also show us things we may prefer not to think about — which is a major reason why many of us slam that door shut on our dreams and try to keep it closed. Those things may include future life problems, or parts of ourselves we tend to ignore or repress, or the larger values and issues involved in a situation we are approaching from a limited point of view.

We may prefer not to think about these matters, but if they are in our dreams, it is because our wiser Self is telling us we *need* to think about them. When our dreams show us future problems, they are also offering tools to avoid or contain those problems — if we will only heed the messages and take appropriate action. When our dreams reveal aspects of ourselves we tend to deny, they invite us to reclaim the energy we waste in denial and to integrate and work with *all* the aspects of our energy. When dreams reflect the bigger issues involved in a current situation, they offer us an inner compass and a corrective to decisions driven by ego or other people's expectations.

When we see things in night dreams we don't like, we need to pay careful attention, because we are being shown elements in our life situation that require understanding and action. The scarier the dream, the more urgent the need to receive its message and figure out what needs to be done.

When you know that, and act accordingly, you'll find your dreams can help you get through the toughest things life throws at you. You'll discover your dreams can help you save your job or your relationship — or move to a better one. They can help you to avoid illness, and the car accident that is otherwise waiting to happen next Tuesday. They can save your life, both your physical life and your life's meaning. To be alive as humans, we need *purpose*, just as we need food and air and sex. Dreams help us remember our life's purpose and live our larger story.

In street talk, when we say, "in your dreams," we are being even more dismissive than when we say "only a dream." *Tu rêves*, on a Paris street, means it can't happen; you're deluding yourself. A guy who tries to pick up an Israeli girl on the beach might be told, "You're dreaming in Spain."

Students of Eastern philosophy often quote the teaching that dreaming is a state of Maya, or illusion (though in Eastern philosophy, waking life is an even more illusory state).

We dismiss dreams, yet the word *dream* has magic. We use it to describe experiences that are hugely important, things that stir the soul and can change the world. *I have a dream*. Martin Luther King may or may not have been inspired by a night dream; by his own earliest account, the numinous moment came when he was leaning over a kitchen sink in the middle of the night, close to despair, and felt the presence of a greater power blessing him and propelling him forward. We all know what he meant. The phrase still sends shivers of recognition through us.

Hollywood is the "dream factory," and the word has long been the most popular in the vocabulary of the advertising business. We are lured by the prospect of acquiring our dream car, our dream appliance, our dream vacation, and our dreamboat (maybe through an online dating service).

So in our usage as well as our understanding, the word *dream* is very slippery. It's illusion or nonsense *and* it's the heart's desire, the secret wish of the soul, a vision for the world.

There's something creepy in the root cellar of the English word *dream*.

When it first appears in Old English, the word *dream* means joy, revelry, or merriment. It can also mean music, or mirthful noise — the kind of merry din you might get if a bunch of medieval topers are downing too many jugs of mead. Other words, ones that look odd to the modern eye (*swefn, maeting*) are used in Old English to mean "dream" in the sense of a vision or an experience during sleep. The word *dream* does not assume those meanings — in general usage — until Chaucer's time. The linguists aren't sure how the shift came about.

Most scholars believe that the word *dream* in the English language today is not the same word as the Old English *dream*, even though the words are spelled the same; the general view is that *dream*, in the sense of a vision or a sleep event, is an import from Old Norse (*draumr*) or Old German (*Traum*). So we need to go tracking in the northlands to find what is hidden in the word *dream*. When we do, we find that *dream* has some tricky relations in the north. One of them is *draugmas*, which means "deception" or "illusion." Another of them — *draugr* — is a ghost, a haunting, or a visitation by the dead. The word *Traum*, contrary to appearances, is not related to *trauma* (which comes from the Greek word for "wound"), but a dream of the *draugr* might indeed be traumatic.

The word *dream* will not stay pinned down, like a big beautiful blue Morpho butterfly that just will not consent to be put under glass.

Many of us, if asked to come up with just one definition for *dream*, would probably talk about images or impressions that appear during sleep. In some European languages the words for "sleep" and "dream" are identical, as in the Latin *somnium*, from which is derived the older French word for dream, *songe*.

Yet for many ancient and indigenous cultures, dreaming is not fundamentally about sleeping; it is about *waking up* — that is, awakening to a larger truth and a larger reality than are accessible to ordinary consciousness.

This is clear in the language of ancient Egypt, which knew a lot about dreaming. The Egyptian word for dream is *rswt*. It literally means "awakening," and in hieroglyphics it often appears followed by a determinative depicted as an open eye.

This makes sense when we reflect that in much of waking life, we can find ourselves in the condition of sleepwalkers, driven by schedules and other people's agendas, too busy or too stressed or too "out of it" to remember what it's all about. The Renaissance physician and alchemist Paracelsus put it like this: "That which the dream shows is the shadow of such wisdom as exists in man, even if during his waking state he may know nothing about it. . . . We do not know it because we are fooling away our time with outward and perishing things, and are asleep in regard to that which is real within ourselves."

For many ancient and indigenous cultures, the dream world is as real — even more real — than everyday waking life. "The dream world is the real world," say the Seneca Iroquois Indians. For most human cultures, across most of history, dreams are of vital importance for two key reasons: they offer a place of encounter between humans and the more-than-human, and they may be prophetic, revealing events that lie in the future.

Both functions of dreaming are possible — in the understanding of our oldest psychology — because in dreams we travel outside the laws of Newtonian physics, and because in dreams, we can receive visitations. This understanding is reflected in the vocabulary of cultures that place a high valuation on dreams.

For example, among the Makiritare, a tribal people of Venezuela, the word for dream is *adekato*, which means a journey of the soul. "When we dream, the spirit goes on walkabout," says a wise woman of the Kukatja, an Aboriginal people of Australia's

Western Desert. Among the Australian Aborigines, personal dreams may be expeditions into the Dreamtime, the place of creation.

Other gifts and powers of dreaming play hide-and-seek in the vocabularies of other peoples. For the Irish, an *aisling* may be a dream, a vision, a poem, or all three. In Hebrew, to dream (*halam*) may also be to bring yourself good health. Among the Iroquois Indians, to dream (*kateraswas*) is to bring yourself good luck, and a dreamer (*atetshents*) is also a shaman, a healer, and a physician.

My favorite definitions of *dream* do not come from dictionaries or cross-cultural analysis. They come — fresh and spontaneous, as new as tomorrow and as ancient as the antlered sorcerer on the wall of a cave near Lascaux — from people everywhere who are tuned into their dreams and honor them.

At a talk at a bookstore in Austin, Texas, I began by asking whether anyone in the audience would care to define the word *dream*. To my surprise, at least thirty hands went up. The first four definitions of a dream offered by the Austin crowd convey a vivid sense of the gifts and possibilities of dreaming:

1. A dream is a beginning.
2. A dream is an adventure.
3. A dream is a message from a wiser self.
4. A dream is a mission.

CHAPTER 2

The NINE POWERS of DREAMING

A dream can be an adventure playground, a jungle gym, a night school (and a flight school), a garden of heavenly delights, a place of encounter with the more-than-human, a portal into the multiverse. A dream is a place, as the Egyptians understood very well. It may be a place of beauty or terror. It can be a place of healing, initiation, higher education, and outrageous fun.

If we are losing our dreams, we are closing off worlds of possibility, entertainment, and learning.

Of all the gifts of dreams, for me the most important are the nine powers of dreaming we'll now unfold.

1. We solve problems in our sleep.
2. Dreams coach us for future challenges and opportunities.
3. Dreams hold up a magic mirror to our actions and behavior.
4. Dreams show us what we need to do to stay well.
5. Dreams are a secret laboratory.

6. Dreams are a creative studio.
7. Dreams help us to mend our divided selves.
8. Dreaming is a key to better relationships.
9. Dreams recall us to our larger purpose.

1. WE SOLVE PROBLEMS IN OUR SLEEP

John Steinbeck observed, "It is a common experience that a problem difficult at night is resolved in the morning after the committee of sleep has worked on it." We may or may not have any recollection of our "committee of sleep" in the morning — we may not even have the slightest recall of a dream — but all of us have had the experience of going to bed with an issue on our mind and finding we had the answer in the morning.

We've been doing this for as long as our kind has been on the planet. We dream in the womb, getting ready for the trauma of coming down the birth canal and of all that life will throw at us after that. As a species — and as individuals — we dream long before we utter our first word.

It's not surprising that creators and innovators often wake up in their dreams to new discoveries and inventions. This is true in every field of human endeavor, from composing great music to fixing the sidewalk.

Dreams help us to soar beyond our current limitations, whatever they are.

Working with the Committee of Sleep

Athena Lou, a dream coach and friend in Hawaii, dreamed she was flying through the air with dolphins and whales. This dream inspired her to leave a secure and well-paid job at a bank and go out on her own, into the riskier field of freelance consulting. In the dream, she reveled in a fabulous sense of freedom, and she decided she needed to claim that same sense of freedom in every part of her life. Now, as a creative consultant, she encourages businesspeople to tune into their dreams, as well as other sources of intuitive knowledge. She has noticed that, more than most people realize, smart business decisions are often guided by dreams.

For instance, an executive in an international high-tech firm dreamed of Oreo cookies flying off into space. The dream inspired her to buy a lot of stock in Nabisco, the manufacturer of Oreos — and the stock price subsequently soared. Then there was a business executive on Oahu who dreamed his company's corporate headquarters was sinking like a ship. The building was tilted at an angle, just like the *Titanic*. He escaped by jumping into an elevator shaft and sliding down the incline, popping out of a window on a lower story as the whole structure came crashing down. The dream led him to go on a job hunt — and he got out just before the company got into deep trouble when the local economy succumbed to a recession.

Dreaming Up *Monster.com*

Jeff Taylor, the creator of the wildly popular internet job search company Monster.com, was inspired by a dream. He woke at 4:30 AM from a dream in which he built an electronic bulletin board system where people could look for jobs. In the dark, he wrote down on a pad next to his bed, "The Monster Board." Nervous that if he went back to sleep he might not be able to decipher or decode what he had written, he went to a coffee shop and proceeded to sketch out a detailed plan.

Notice that Taylor was prepared for his guiding dream in two ways. First, he had already been thinking and feeling his way toward a major innovation. Second, he was ready to catch his dream — on the pad by the bed — and to act right away on its guidance.

Dreaming Bouncy Sidewalks

For two decades, Richard Valeriano's job as a Santa Monica street inspector included checking for damage to sidewalks caused by the spreading roots of the city's shade trees. Broken concrete is expensive to repair and a frequent source of injuries to pedestrians. Work crews in Santa Monica were being sent out with chain saws to cut down mature ficus trees.

One night after work Valeriano dreamed of a bouncy, flexible sidewalk that solved the problem. "In my dream, sidewalks were all bending and twisting, but there was no cracking. I woke up and said, 'Wow! Elastic sidewalks! I wonder how we can make them?'"

He did not know how to enact the dream until his health club, during remodeling, installed rubber tiles as flooring. This inspired Valeriano to look for a company willing to develop a prototype for a rubber sidewalk. The tiles were made from recycled auto tires, and the city of Santa Monica tested them by having bicyclists, Rollerbladers, and women in stiletto heels, among others, do their worst.

Five years later, rubber walkways were being tried out in sixty American cities. The rubber was saving the shade trees and pedestrians' footing. Rubber walkways were installed in April 2006 around the willow oaks on Rhode Island Avenue in Washington, DC. The kids liked the bounce — though they find it's not so easy to carve your initials or draw on the pavement in chalk.

Solve It in Your Sleep

Here's a plan for any night of the year:

Before you hit the sack, write down an intention for the night. A simple way is to fill in the blank in the following statement: "I would like guidance on. . . ."

Make sure you are ready to record whatever comes to you —

and be ready to do so whenever you happen to wake up, because the *big* messages often come at unsocial hours. Many great discoveries are made between 3 AM and 4 AM, which is also the hour (according to some surveys) when most babies are born and most people die.

If you wake up and you do not recall any dream, relax. Wiggle around in bed. Sometimes a dream comes back as you get your body into the position you were in when you were dreaming. If you still don't remember a dream, write down whatever you are thinking and feeling. You may find you have the gift of the dream — a solution or an inspiration — even if you have lost the content of the dream.

On a spring morning in 1905, Einstein woke up with a theory that revolutionized science, the Special Theory of Relativity. He had told a friend the previous day he felt he was on the verge of a huge breakthrough but was not sure what it was. In the morning, he had all of it, fresh and sparkling in his mind. There is no evidence Einstein remembered the content of his dreams from that tremendous night, but he received their gift, and it changed everything.

The lesson is clear. Whatever problem we have to deal with, from the carpool schedule to a scientific Theory of Everything, *we can solve it in our sleep*.

2. DREAMS COACH US FOR FUTURE CHALLENGES AND OPPORTUNITIES

Our dreams are constantly coaching us for challenges and opportunities that lie ahead of us on the road of life. It's possible that we rehearse *everything* that will take place in the future in our dreams, though we forget most of it.

Across human evolution, dreaming has been a vital survival mechanism. It is likely that in the days when our ancestors were naked hominids without good weapons, their dream radar — their ability to scout across both space and time — often enabled them to avoid becoming breakfast for saber-toothed tigers and other hungry predators.

A recent theory posits that dreaming prepares us for challenges by putting us through frequent workouts in *threat simulation*, helping us to develop the reflexes and responses that will get us through.

This is good, but I suspect our relationship with the future in dreams is much deeper and more important than this. I believe that in dreaming, we have access to the matrix in which the events and circumstances that will manifest in our physical lives have their origins. We not only *see* future events; we can *choose* — to varying degrees, and according to our level of consciousness — which among many possible future events will manifest.

It's my impression that we are dreaming the future all the time.

If you are not yet aware you are doing this, consider the times you have had the experience of déjà vu. I have yet to meet someone who has *never* had that feeling of encountering a person or a place for the first time — in ordinary reality — and *knowing* you have seen them before. Most often déjà vu is experienced when waking events resemble something we have dreamed. We may have forgotten the dream, but when a physical event catches up with it, recognition stirs from a deep memory bank.

If you adopt the practice of recording your dreams and comparing the dream data with subsequent events, it won't take long for you to notice some matchups. The incidents you preview in your dreams may be trivial or terrifying, blah or wonderful. They may be events in your own life, or events in the future history of the world.

In our dreams, we have several kinds of engagement with the future.

Precognitive Dreams

Through *precognition*, we see events and circumstances ahead of time, as they will be played out. A precognitive dream may be literal or symbolic or both. For example, a dream of a tsunami might turn out to be both a preview of a literal disaster and advance notice of an emotional storm that will hit with the force of a tsunami. We may not understand what we have seen in a precognitive dream until a physical event catches up with that dream. It may also be difficult for us to understand what we have seen because we are looking at things from a certain angle, perhaps the perspective of a different person. But with practice, we can learn to recognize markers that a dream relates to future events, and we can then move to clarify and use the dream information.

Such practice becomes very interesting when our dreams show us possible future events that can be changed for the better. We may call such dreams *early advisories*; they may be *early warnings* or early signals of coming *opportunities*.

Early-Warning Dreams

Some dreams are *early warnings* of a possible future problem — a crisis at work, the bust-up of a relationship, a health problem, a car accident. We may not want to focus on any of these unpleasant possibilities. But if we are willing to study what an early-warning dream is telling us, we will often find that it is giving us vital information that can help us avoid the problem if we take appropriate action.

Here's a simple, everyday example: Cara dreamed that a good friend pulled up beside her on the right side of her car and pointed at the front right tire, signaling that there was something wrong. On waking, Cara inspected the passenger side of her car — something she was otherwise unlikely to do — and found that the fairly new right front tire was flat. The dream advisory enabled her to take care of the problem immediately and get on her way safely without a major hassle.

Sometimes we dream the future for the benefit of another person, or even of a great cause. What will then happen depends on whether we can find an effective way to get the dream information to the person who can best act upon it. What follows is an example of a dream that changed history when it was passed on to the right person.

The Dream That Saved the First Roman Emperor

Rome may never have had emperors but for a dream that saved the life of Octavian, Julius Caesar's great-nephew. In 42 BCE — in a scene made famous by Shakespeare's play *Julius Caesar* — Octavian and Mark Antony commanded legions that were gathered at Philippi, in Macedonia, to avenge Caesar's murder. Arrayed against the army of Octavian and Mark Antony in strong defensive positions were the forces of Brutus and Cassius, the murderers of Caesar who called themselves liberators of Rome. Before the first battle of Philippi, Octavian was ill and exhausted in his tent. He was roused by a friend who told him he had dreamed that Octavian would be killed in a surprise attack unless he left his tent at once. Octavian heeded the dream warning, fled from his tent — and so escaped being stabbed to death soon after when Brutus's soldiers burst in and plunged their swords into his camp bed, shredding it to ribbons, under the impression that the boy general was still in it. Octavian and Mark Antony were victorious in the second battle of Phlippi, and Octavian became Augustus, the first Roman emperor.

Early-Opportunity Dreams

Early-opportunity dreams may also require action if we are going to manifest a future we'll enjoy. You dream you are in your ideal home, or doing the work that nourishes your soul and your bank account, or you are with your soul mate, who is someone you have not yet met in the regular world. These dreams may be inspiring and encouraging, and you don't want to let them float away like helium balloons. You'll want to figure out what practical action you can take to move decisively in the direction of these happy dreams.

Any future we can see (in dreams or through wakeful intuition) is a *possible* future, and we can influence the odds on the manifestation of a specific future event. While it may seem impossible for an individual to change certain future events perceived in dreams — like a natural disaster or death at an advanced age — it may still be possible to work with the dream information in a useful way: for example, to alert friends not to go on vacation in the place where the dreamed hurricane will hit, or to help someone whose death is near, and their family, to meet that situation with grace and closure.

Dream Seers

In most human cultures across history, dreamers who provide reliable information about events at a distance in time have been highly valued. When their visions have involved the possible destinies of nations and armies, they have been called seers and prophets.

In Spain, in the time of Philip II, a young noblewoman named Lucrecia de León became renowned as a *vidente* (seer) and a prophet. Her gifts were first revealed when, at age twelve, she accurately described a royal funeral procession in Badajoz; weeks later, news reached her family home in Madrid that Anne of Austria, Philip's queen, had died in Badajoz as the royal couple were traveling to Portugal. Later Lucrecia dreamed the destruction of the Spanish Armada and the death of its admiral a year before those events.

In her dreams, she functioned as a psychic spy, secretly traveling to the home of Sir Francis Drake in England to eavesdrop on the plans of Spain's enemies. She often roamed the palace of Philip II at night, picking up details of court intrigues. Her information was considered so valuable and so time sensitive by the head of the powerful Mendoza clan that he arranged to have a cleric record Lucrecia's dream reports every morning while an armed courier waited to rush them on horseback to his master.

While some of Lucrecia's veridical dreams are cases of precognition (the wreck of the Spanish Armada), others are more likely examples of traveling clairvoyance, in which her consciousness was projected across space to view synchronous events happening at a distance. What is remarkable is that she was able to move through time, in her dreams, in very much the same way that she could travel across space.

I believe this is true not only for a seer like Lucrecia de León, but for all of us. When we go dreaming, we travel in time — to the past as well as the future — in much the same way that we are accustomed, in physical life, to traveling in space.

Time Is a Kind of Space

As dreamers, we discover and inhabit the true nature of time, as it has always been known to dream travelers and is now confirmed by modern science. Linear time, as measured by clocks and experienced in plodding sequences of one thing following another, always heading in the same direction, is an illusion of limited human awareness, at best (as Einstein said), a convenience. In dreaming, as in heightened states of consciousness, we step into a more spacious time, and we can move forward or backward at varying speeds. We can also step off a particular event track onto a parallel time track that may also be a parallel universe.

A medieval scholastic, trying to account for Lucrecia's time-tripping, might say, "She stepped into the Aevum." The Aevum, in Thomist theology, is an in-between realm between eternity (the divine depth beyond time) and the corrupted world where humans live in sequential time. In the Aevum, duration is not determined by linear time but by movements of consciousness.

This is a medieval version of what has become a very modern idea: that if we can step outside our consensual hallucinations, we'll discover that time is actually the fourth dimension of space. As H. G. Wells's Time Traveler says, with wonderful clarity, "Scientific people know very well that Time is only a kind of Space."

Viewed from the fourth dimension, past, present, and future are in fact simultaneous and only experienced sequentially because of our mental perception of them. In the dream state the mind is not shackled in this way and is able to move between situations and probable events in the past and future with equal mobility.

But hold on for a minute — doesn't this mean that though we can travel to the past and future, we can't change them? That's how Wells's Time Traveler views the situation in *The Time Machine*. He regards our many selves at different moments in time — our baby self, our teen self, our current self, our geriatric self, and so on — as three-dimensional "cross sections" of our larger four-dimensional identity, "which is a fixed and unalterable thing."

Much as I love *The Time Machine*, I must observe that time travel in dreams is more interesting than this. We not only travel to past and future; we travel between alternate timelines. With growing awareness, we can develop greater and greater ability to *choose* the event track — maybe one of infinite alternative possible event tracks — that will be followed through a certain life passage, or even the larger history of our world. This may be a case of the "observer effect" operating on a human scale. It is well understood that at quantum levels, deep within subatomic space, the act of observation plucks a specific phenomenon out of a bubbling cauldron of possibilities. It may be so in the cauldron of our dreaming: through the act of observation, we select a certain event track that will begin to be manifested in the physical world. By a fresh act of observation, or re-visioning, we can then proceed to alter that event track, or switch to an entirely different one.

Dreaming Can Save Your Life

Let's get serious about the survival aspect of dreams: they can save your life.

I once dreamed I was driving up a hill in Troy, New York, heading east. As I approached a fork in the road, everything stopped. I then entered a series of new scenes in extraordinary locales, and became aware that I was traveling through a series of afterlife transitions. When I came out of the dream, I knew I had to take special note of the place — near the fork in the road — where the action took place, because (in my personal mode of dreaming) entry into afterlife situations in this way is a signal that literal death is a possibility.

Three weeks later, driving up that hill in Troy, I noticed that a delivery truck parked on the right side of the road had created a blind spot. Remembering the dream, instead of pulling out to pass the van, I slowed almost to a stop. This may have saved my life when an eighteen-wheeler came barreling down the hill at sixty or seventy miles per hour, hogging the whole road beside the parked van.

We not only get advisories days or weeks before a possible future event; we can get an early warning dream *decades* before events start to catch up with it. The case of Celia is highly instructive.

In her youth, Celia, a woman from Upstate New York, dreamed that while she was driving a bright red truck she crashed into the rock face of a sheered mountain. She died in the dream and woke feeling that it was a premonition of a physical event. She took the dream very seriously and heeded its warning. Though she loved red cars (and trucks), for twenty years she didn't buy one and avoided riding in a red vehicle because of her dream.

Twenty years on, she still remembered the dream, but thought she had traveled far enough in life to have left behind the danger it foreshadowed. She bought a red car — not a red truck — and determined to be careful. She was fine in the red car. It grew old and she replaced it with a white car. Another ten years went by. She divorced and began a relationship with a new friend, who had a red truck. As she was driving through the mountains in her friend's truck one fall, Celia veered to the side of the road to avoid a deer.

She looked up and saw the sheered-off rock face of a mountain a few feet away.

It was the dream.

Because she remembered her dream, she knew what to do. Her dream recollection guided her lightning-fast reflexes. She wrenched the wheel violently, turning as hard as she could. The red truck scraped along the side of the rock; doors and bumpers were torn away, but Celia walked away from the accident. Thirty years after the dream, her recollection of its exact details — and the way that it prompted her to act immediately to prevent the worst part of the dream playing out — saved Celia's life.

3. DREAMS HOLD UP A MAGIC MIRROR TO OUR ACTIONS AND BEHAVIOR

Have you ever dreamed that you looked at yourself in a mirror and noticed you were quite different from the way you think of yourself in waking life? While we look in a mirror in some of our dreams, the dream is also looking at us. The whole of a dream

may function as a mirror in a larger sense, showing us sides of
ourselves and our behavior that we may prefer not to see, or have
simply been shutting out, in ordinary reality.

A great game to play with many dreams is to compare the behavior of our dream self with our waking self. If you are wimp-
ing out of situations in your dreams, passively following courses
others set for you, or tending to remain an observer when action
might be desirable, then you'll want to ask yourself where in waking life you have a tendency to behave that way. If you are forever
catching a bus (a collective vehicle that runs according to other
people's schedules and makes lots of stops that have no interest
for you), you may want to ask yourself how often in waking life
you submit to agendas that are not of your making and don't allow
you to give your best.

Alternatively, if you find you have strength and magical powers in your dreams that you generally do *not* exhibit in waking life,
you'll want to try to reach into the dreamspace and bring those
powers through, to work for you in your physical life.

Funhouse and Magnifying Mirrors

If what we see in the mirror of dreams sometimes seems like a
funhouse freak show or the work of a Hollywood special effects
crew, it's because we've been failing to look at something we need
to see. The drama and the magnification ensure we pay better attention.

During a dream workshop on a chilly fall day in Madison,
Wisconsin, three people in succession shared dreams that reminded me of the image of the Lightning-Struck Tower in tarot
— an image of violent, unavoidable, and unwanted change, bringing the overthrow of established structures.

Despite the similarity in mood and imagery in these dreams,
each dream brought a distinctively personal message (this is true

of *all* dreams, which is why we should never go to dream dictionaries for their meanings).

In her dream, Bea was terrified by jet fighters swooping down from the sky, firing rockets. She rushed into an underground concrete bunker, only to realize, to her dismay, that nothing could be done to fix the situation from down there. I asked her whether she ever had a tendency to behave in waking life the way she had done in the dream. She was a quick study. She rapidly identified both work and family situations in which she tended to "hide in a bunker," leaving problems unsolved. Her action plan was to stand up — and speak up — for herself.

Liz dreamed she was on the porch of her childhood home with close family. She watched five old propeller planes fly by in military formation. Then an enormous modern jet fighter swooped down. She knew it was coming down and would destroy the old neighborhood. As we talked about the dream, Liz recognized that it might be telling her that it was time for old structures to come down.

A third dreamer in that workshop shared a dream in which a lightning bolt hit the roof of her car while she was driving. The car in the dream was her actual car, and she recognized the location, so we discussed the need for her to use the dream as a literal advisory to be careful on that road in the event of a thunderstorm. We also explored the question of what might be coming up in the dreamer's life that would strike with the force of lightning.

Magnifying mirror dreams often show us strong emotions moving with the power of natural forces — rage or grief may erupt like a volcano, or tear up the neighborhood like a twister, or drown the whole scene like a tsunami. Working with such dreams, we want to remember that they may relate *both* to a literal phenomenon *and* to an emotional or symbolic condition. Indeed, sometimes a dream previews a literal event that will also have great symbolic resonance for the dreamer. We need to take dreams

more literally, and the events of waking life more symbolically —
which is the theme of part 2.

Dreams Show Us Our Life Roads —
and How We Are Driving

Our dream mirrors reflect how we are conducting ourselves on
the roads of life. If you see yourself driving too fast in a dream,
that may be an advisory to slow down and pay closer attention to
what is ahead of you and around you — when you are at the
wheel, and also in other ways.

Maybe the road you are on, in a dream, ends with a ROAD
CLOSED sign or an impassable obstacle. Then you'll want to consider whether the road you are on is actually going where you
think you are headed.

Watching your dream mirror is the antidote for going through
life with your eyes fixed on the *rearview* mirror — which is what
many of us tend to do, trapped in personal history and old patterns and issues.

In showing us how we are driving as we go *forward* in life, the
dream mirror can give us very exact guidance. I dreamed I was
driving fast and smoothly and felt very confident. I sped down to
a crossing where a yellow drawbridge opened and closed at rapid
intervals. Because I was going so fast, I missed the right moment
to make the crossing. As I drove onto the drawbridge, it was going
up. The car slowed as the gradient steepened and — unlike a
movie hero in a chase sequence — I knew I did not have the speed
and power to jump the car across the gap. I realized I would need
to back up to give myself momentum, and time my crossing very
precisely to get over while the drawbridge was down — or be able
to make the jump when the gap was not too wide.

I do not intend to use this as a *literal* advisory on approaching a bridge! But I was able to use it, in very helpful ways, as an

advisory on approaching a more important crossing in my life. I understood from the dream that I would need to temper my frequent tendency to charge ahead with careful attention to timing and developing the necessary resources to bring a project to fruition.

Dreaming and Course Correction

Mirror dreams recall us to fundamental values when we are being pushed and pulled by rival pressures and agendas, and in this way help us to make necessary course corrections.

Carl Jung tells an illuminating story about how a businessman got clarity on the ethics of a certain situation. The night after receiving an attractive proposition, the businessman dreamed that his hands and forearms were covered with disgusting black dirt. Though reluctant to relate the dream to waking circumstances, he accepted that the dream was a warning that he was in danger of getting involved in "dirty business" and bowed out of the deal.

The Bible contains a marvelous story of a dream that invited a king to make a course correction. In his dream, Nebuchadnezzar saw a tree that grew all the way up to heaven, and he gave orders to chop down the tree but leave the roots intact. Daniel warned him about hubris, but Nebuchadnezzar disregarded the caution, with disastrous results.

The dream advisory on the need for course correction may come in less dramatic ways.

Dave, an airplane mechanic, shared his personal version of the very familiar "late for class" dream. A recurring theme in his dreams was that he was trying to get to class on time, but felt his legs dragging, as if fettered or coated with cement.

We've all had that "legs in cement" feeling. I get it when I am pushing myself — or letting others push me — to do something that in my heart I really don't want to do. Dave agreed, after discussion, that he would think about ways in his life in which he might be struggling to get to the wrong class, and how he might want to shift his focus.

Jack was expending a great deal of energy trying to stay in a situation that had become very conflicted and was draining him both emotionally and financially. Then shortly before the November 2006 U.S. elections, he dreamed that Secretary of Defense Donald Rumsfeld was hiding out at his house. Rumsfeld was weary and sick, and, wearing his pinstripe suit, he got into bed with Jack. Jack said he was aware in the dream that "I don't feel this is right."

Jack had once admired Don Rumsfeld and thought him a brilliant man, but he had become strongly opposed to the Iraq War and Rumsfeld's policy of "staying the course." Looking into the mirror of this dream, Jack concluded: "I have to get out of this situation. If I try to stay the course, I'll end up hemorrhaging blood and money."

In the dream mirror, we not only see how we are driving, but when to take a different road. Our dream mirror offers us the great gift of *objectivity*. Its pictures do not lie. They carry us beyond the illusions and idées fixes of the little everyday mind. This is especially true of the dreams we do not ask for or do not want.

Mirror dreams not only compensate for lopsided attitudes and offer course correction; they serve the role of conscience. Dostoyevsky's *Crime and Punishment* is a marvelous case study in the dreams of conscience. While the demented student Raskolnikov is growing fantastic daydreams as he plots a terrible crime, his true dreams hold up the mirror that shows him the evil of his designs.

4. DREAMS SHOW US WHAT WE NEED TO DO TO STAY WELL

Dreaming is medicine. This is true in ways that are easily evidenced by medical data. For example, clinical studies strongly suggest that people suffering from symptoms of depression start to recover when dream function increases — as monitored by brain waves and/or the length of the phases of rapid-eye-movement (REM) sleep — and that they experience a decisive shift for the better when they increase their dream recall and their sharing of dreams. One of the physicians who works closely with me, Dr. Robert Weissberg, sometimes says to depressive patients, "I will be happy to prescribe medication for you, if it is needed, but I also want you to bring a dream or two to our next meeting." He has noticed that the patients who are most successful in remembering dreams are often the ones who experience the most rapid improvement in their condition.

Let's be clear about what dreams mean for our health.

We have a personal physician who can give us an *impeccable* diagnosis of our physical, mental, emotional, and spiritual condition and can tell us what we need to stay well. If we are ailing, the same doctor will give us the right prescription — and in addition to this, can offer us powerful images our body can use in the direction of self-healing. This personal physician is also a healer, therapist, and friend who works tirelessly to support our well-being. This doctor, amazingly, is also a movie producer who stages brilliant dramatic productions that show us how to follow the natural path of our energy.

The dream doctor is willing to make house calls at any hour and doesn't charge a cent.

Why would we ever refuse the service and friendship of a physician like this?

Dreams Diagnose Possible Problems Before Physical Symptoms Are Detected

Our bodies know what is going on inside them, and they speak to us about this in dreams, which often diagnose developing illness before physical symptoms are detected. By working with these diagnostic dreams, we can often deal with a problem before it has reached a critical phase — and sometimes avoid painful and costly medical interventions.

Some of our dreamscapes are living dioramas of what is going on inside our bodies. Conflicts taking place in our dreams are sometimes dramatic portrayals of how our immune system is trying to cope — or failing to cope — with disease. Dreams can take us deep into the cellular structures of the body. For thousands of years, gifted physicians have recognized that such "bodytalk" dreams can provide accurate diagnosis of our ailments, often long before physical symptoms can be observed.

Reading somatic messages in this way was central to traditional Chinese medicine, as well as to medical practice in ancient Greece and in many other cultures. In the Victorian era, Western doctors continued to look for diagnostic information in their patients' dreams.

In her late thirties, Ellen dreamed that a threatening intruder walked into her dream house and pointed a gun at her breast. She was sensitive to dream imagery and knew intuitively that the dream was warning her that she might have developed breast cancer. She immediately sought medical help. Ellen's cancer was discovered in its earliest stages, thanks to the fact that she remembered her dream and acted on its warning, and her problem was solved with a simple lumpectomy.

Sensing that her dreams were telling her about a serious health problem, Carol made repeated visits to a physician who was initially baffled by her punch list of vague and elusive symptoms. The doctor began to question whether there was really a physical problem. Then Carol dreamed a very simple dream — a large wolf appeared and spoke to her: "I am Lupus Wolf." Carol called the next morning, snagged an appointment, and told her physician the dream. Now he went to work and soon confirmed that her dream diagnosis was exactly correct; she had lupus.

Dreams Show Us the Natural Path of Our Energy

The dream of Lupus Wolf gave Carol more than diagnostic information her physician could work with to help her get well. Lupus Wolf became a guide and partner in her dreams, helping her to become an active participant in her own healing. He showed her the foods she needed to eat, warned her away from a medicine that would cause anxiety, and led her in further dreams to a healing garden, a place she found she could revisit to relax and imagine herself well.

Sarah dreamed she was at her family place with her therapist, a Tibetan Buddhist, and a team of monks. She wanted to cook up a meat dish and needed more beef. Her therapist and the monks refused to supply this. A huge wildcat — a cross between a tiger and a panther — irrupted into the scene and ripped the back off a silly little spaniel. In discussion, Sarah realized that the Big Cat was attacking the part of her that had a tendency to behave like a "pet" — and she needed to be fed and nourished in ways that her current practice and family situation did not provide. She resolved to "get to the meat" by feeding her Big Cat at lunch, and she would then see what happened if she called on that energy in family situations.

Whatever our condition, the state and behavior of animals in our dreams is often a remarkable guide to what we need to do to follow the natural path of our energy — what we need to eat, how we need to move (or lie still), and how we need to read and interact with others.

Dreams Give Us the Right Prescriptions

Dreams offer us prescriptions that may or may not require a doctor's signature, and they help us to make good choices between alternative practitioners and practices.

A woman dreamer asked her night dreams for guidance about whether she should have surgery for a herniated disk. In her dream, she saw a zippy fifties roadster, painted red and white, with a huge ultramodern sound system in the back. A mechanic told her in the dream that mechanical repairs were not necessary and would be excessively costly. Waking, she recognized that her body was the fifties roadster, and that a sound system is also a disk player. She proceeded to experiment — with very healing results — with the power of toning and vibration to help with her back problem.

Five months before she was diagnosed with a serious form of breast cancer, Nancy dreamed she was searching for three white tigers that needed help. A man in law enforcement helped her track them down. Following Nancy's intuition, they located the tigers, while the man used his formal training and strength to help the animals. Nancy met the law enforcement man from her dream in waking life five months later; he was her oncologist. The dream guided her to work with his formal skills while continuing to draw on her own intuition.

Dreams help us to tell the difference between what is medicine and what is poison for our system (and a particular Rx may be either or both) — sometimes quite literally.

When my friend Wanda Burch was a child, her father dreamed that a prescribed tonic was poison. When her mom came home with the prescription, her father grabbed the bottle and drove back to the pharmacy, demanding that it be tested. There had been a mix-up; the tonic was rat poison.

An elderly woman named Mary received an equally serious warning about a prescription. In her dream, she walked into a pharmacy and watched the druggist pouring pills into a bottle. Mary opened the cap and tumbled one of the pills into her hand. She turned it over and was horrified to see a skull and crossbones on the back.

A few days later, a physician changed Mary's usual prescription to one he thought would work better for her. When she went into the pharmacy with the prescription, she found she was inside her dream. She opened the bottle she was given, examined the contents and felt certain she was looking at the poison pill from her dream. She went back to her doctor and insisted on returning to her previous medication.

Sometimes the dream Rx is for a natural remedy. Troubled by hypertension, Cara dreamed that a charming chef appeared in her kitchen and cooked her a delicious breakfast of oatmeal with raspberries on top. Inspired by her dream, Cara went to the grocery store the next day, purchased the necessary supplies, and started eating oatmeal with raspberries for breakfast — and her blood pressure came down.

Dreams Give Us Imagery for Self-Healing

Dreams are a wonderful source of fresh, spontaneous imagery for healing — imagery the body believes because it comes from deep within ourselves. Dream images are more powerful than prefabricated visualization scripts because they are our own material, produced especially for us.

Dreams show us our conditions — physical, emotional, mental, and spiritual — in a different language from the medical profession (though they may also incorporate medical language and medical procedures). Dreams offer us the power of visioning and *naming* our symptoms in ways that help us to become well.

In Dreams, We Have Access to Direct Healing

Wanda Burch, whose book *She Who Dreams* is the best guide I know to dream healing, had a recent experience of direct healing through a dream. A doctor looked at a mole on the sole of her left foot and determined that it needed to be removed. This would require minor surgery that would cause some residual pain for a few days.

Prior to the scheduled surgery, Wanda approached sleep with the strong thought, "Why do I have to go through this? Isn't there another way?"

In her dream, she inspected the mole on the sole of her foot. Then a hand appeared from nowhere — as if out of a cloud — holding a large black pencil. The hand drew a circle around the mole, and the mole popped off and disappeared.

In the morning, Wanda looked at the sole of her foot. No trace of the mole. She looked at her other foot, thinking she must be confused. No mole. She got her husband to look, and he confirmed what had happened: a dream event had delivered immediate physical healing. Her husband insisted she should keep her medical appointment, so the doctors could learn from this.

On several very critical nights in my life, I have received direct healing from a being who appears as a bear. On one of these nights, I found myself in leather armor, leading warriors who marched under the banner of a bear goddess. Exhausted by battles, I wandered away into the wilderness, ready to die. A bear cub came to me and led me to a place of healing where a great Mother Bear cracked my ribcage, cleansed my heart and lungs, and replaced them after lining the cavity with soft green moss. In the morning, I felt deeply cleansed and refreshed — and *blessed*.

Dream healing is available, any night. We just need to ask. The ancients journeyed from all over the Mediterranean littoral to the temples of dream healing associated with Asklepios and his father, Apollo, not just to seek dream diagnosis but in hopes of a direct and full experience of healing in a night vision. Such experiences may happen in spontaneous dreams and are immense blessings. We can *invite* the presence of the sacred healer into our nights and our lives. We can simply say, "I ask for healing." Or we can say, like the ancient Greek orator Aelius Aristides, who walked very close to his god, "I ask for the health my body requires to serve the purposes of the soul."

It's always okay to ask for help, in our animate universe —
but also always a good idea to ask nicely.

5. DREAMS ARE A SECRET LABORATORY

Wolfgang Pauli (1900–1958) was an extraordinary scientist, a
Nobel laureate who formulated the "exclusion principle," which
explains why matter does not collapse on itself and which remains
one of the foundations of contemporary physics. Fellow Nobel
Prize–winning physicist Max Born thought that Pauli's genius ex-
ceeded even that of Einstein.

Pauli wrote that, across his whole life, dreams were his "secret laboratory." When the role of dreams in the history of science
and innovation is discussed, we are generally given a sampling of
one-off dream images that have inspired or contributed to a major
discovery. Inventor Elias Howe had a dream that showed him
where to put the hole in the sewing machine needle; scientist
Friedrich August von Kekulé had a hypnagogic vision that revealed the shape of the benzene ring; the archaeologist Hermann
Hilprecht dreamed an ancient Assyrian priest showed him how
the parts of a mysterious artifact fitted together. Such examples
are interesting and even extraordinary, but they do not take us
where we need to go, which is into that "secret laboratory" where
Pauli and other great innovative minds have always worked. The
engagement of our greatest scientists with the realm of dream and
imagination can be presented as a set of particulars, but it is also
a wave function and a constant.

If we want to understand how deep this engagement can go,
Pauli's correspondence with Jung is a very good place to start. Between 1932 and 1958, the brilliant physicist and the no-less-
brilliant psychologist traded questing and detailed letters in which
they helped each other to explore the interweavings of mind and
matter at every level of the multiverse. Jung sent Pauli early drafts

of his paper on synchronicity, and he rewrote it (not as radically as Pauli would have liked) under the physicist's razor-edged critiques. Pauli sent Jung dream upon dream over all those years, and papers (like his "Background Physics") in which he discussed how his dreams guided his inquiries into everything. Pauli, who was twenty-five years younger than Jung, first approached the Swiss psychologist for counsel during a personal crisis when he was thirty. In the first two years of their acquaintance, he shared thirteen hundred dream reports with Jung and his assistant. This gives us an idea of the sheer volume of Pauli's remembered dreaming. Tracking the evolution of Pauli's dream symbols and dream characters, Jung developed his own theories of how dreaming opens a path to self-realization (or "individuation").

Pauli's dreams coached him on his scientific work, and in dreams he frequently found himself holding discussions with colleagues — especially Einstein and Niels Bohr — that took them beyond their current level of understanding. His dreams also took him into other areas of study, such as philology. He shared with Jung a dream that drove him to study the etymology of the word *window* (which derives from "wind-eye") and how coincidence came into play in his research, putting him next to a distinguished linguist he had never met before, in a chance encounter on a tram.

Beyond specific discoveries, Pauli's dreams helped him to recognize and pursue a lifelong project that was of even greater importance than his contributions to quantum physics. That project was a unified theory that would explain that there is no separation between psyche and physics at any level of reality. Its nature became clear to him in his midthirties, when he dreamed that Einstein came to him and told him that quantum theory was one-dimensional but reality was two dimensional. In the dream encounter, Pauli realized he must accept a new dimension of reality, the psychospiritual depth of things. "I have come to accept the existence of deeper spiritual layers that cannot be adequately defined by the conventional concept of time," Pauli wrote Jung. The driving theme in his later work is the search for the common fundament of mind and matter, and the union of physics and psychology.

Pauli's quest was supported by the rich play of coincidence around him. He was a troubled genius, and his roiling emotions may explain what became known as the Pauli Effect. In Pauli's presence, expensive laboratory equipment had a tendency to break down or blow up. This happened with a cyclotron that had just been installed at Princeton when Pauli arrived on the scene. Pauli came to enjoy his own legend for producing dramatic psycho-kinetic effects. The play of dreamlike symbols and unlikely con-junctions in his physical life confirmed his "working hypothesis" of "the essential identity of the *mundus archetypus* and physis."

Let's add four quick scenes from the larger story of dreaming in the history of science, invention, and discovery.

Scene One: Dreaming Up Cryptography

Johannes Trithemius, a medieval abbot of Sponheim, is now re-garded, because of the codes contained in his *Stegonagraphia*, as the founder of modern cryptography. Trithemius attributed his career as scholar and cleric to a powerful dream he experienced at fifteen, in which he was shown two tablets — one containing visual images, one written texts — and told to choose between them. He chose the tablet with the writing, and (having been near-illiterate up to this point) became a brilliant and industrious scholar versed in many languages and capable of inventing com-plex codes and word games. Since he was also a magus, his ap-proach to secret communications went beyond word tricks. He recorded the evocations that could summon spirits to collect mes-sages and transport them to the intended recipients.

The nascent British intelligence service was not slow to see the potential. In 1562, the magus John Dee spent ten days at the Golden Angel tavern in Antwerp, transcribing the complex texts of the German abbot from a borrowed manuscript. He then reported to William Cecil — who was in the process of setting up an intelligence service for Queen Elizabeth I — reporting that he had possession of a key to the "secret sciences."

Scene Two: Dreaming the First Military Aircraft

J. W. Dunne became celebrated in the 1920s for his *An Experiment with Time*, in which he chronicled a series of precognitive dreams and speculated that there are many — possibly infinite — experiences of time. In his later work, he offered the hypothesis that precognitive dreams may be *caused* by future events.

Dunne was also a soldier, a pilot, and one of the pioneers of military aviation. He designed and built Britain's first military aircraft, a tailless plane with a V-shaped wing, according to principles that are still in use in Stealth technology.

The origin of Dunne's interest in aircraft design is a fascinating story of how the play of dreams and imagination on a young mind can carry through into remarkable adult achievement. In his early teens, he read Jules Verne's story, "Clipper of the Clouds," which described a flying machine that looked very much like a ship, driven by screw propellers and without wings. A few days after reading the story, the boy Dunne dreamed he had invented his own flying machine, very different from Verne's. In the dream, he was flying among the clouds seated in "a tiny open boat constructed of some whitish material on a wooden framework." This contraption corresponded to nothing he had ever seen or heard about.

"I never forgot that dream," Dunne later recalled. He thought about it when he was on sick leave after the Boer War and was assigned by the War Office to work on devising "some heavier-than-air contrivance, which should solve the great military problem of reconnaissance." In 1910, he succeeded in making a test flight of his plane with the V-shaped wing. The pilot sat at the point of the V, in a boatlike structure composed of canvas stretched over wooden struts. Sitting in this as he flew over the fields, Dunne had the impression of "traveling through the void in a simple, open canoe" — and realized he was now living out a dream from twenty years before.

Scene Three: Agassiz Dreams the Fish behind the Fossil

When the great zoologist Louis Agassiz was working on a classification of all known fossil fish, he found he could not identify a specimen encased in a stone slab. He could not risk extracting the fossil from the stone for fear of destroying it. Then, three nights in succession he dreamed of seeing the fish in perfect original condition, as it might have been swimming in the sea millions of years ago. He was too dozy to capture his impressions on the first two nights, but on the third night he had pen and paper by the bed and disciplined himself to draw the ancient fish in the dark, when he was still half inside the dream. When he compared his drawing with the specimen, he was certain he had dreamed true.

Scene Four: A Railroad Baron's Brownies

Arthur Stilwell was one of the great financiers and railroad barons of nineteenth-century America. He made a fortune and lost it, but his name — as in Stilwell Financial — is still associated with Janus mutual funds and the Kansas City Southern Railroad. However, whether laying railroad track or founding a city in Texas — Port Arthur — Stilwell often took his inspiration from dreams. Today, Port Arthur acknowledges its origins on its official city website with the following statement: "The inspiration for Port Arthur's founding was novel; railroad pioneer Arthur E. Stilwell, who established the town, later wrote that the ideas for his railways and the location of his namesake city came from 'brownies' who spoke to him."

Stilwell himself kept quiet about these things until the end of his business career, concerned that his respectable investors would consider him a "nut" if he revealed that he was laying railroad track according to plans that were being given to him in his dreams. In 1921, Stilwell confessed that he had been visited in his sleep throughout his heyday by guides that (like Robert Louis Stevenson) he called Brownies. In dreams these beings gave him the plans for his railroads, the location and layout of the city of Port Arthur, and the spur to embark on many other business ventures, as well as ideas for books. Stilwell wrote: "There is no doubt in my mind that these messages come from the spirit world, and that this circle of spirits that communicates with me by this rare method is comprised of engineers, poets, and authors."

There's that "committee of sleep" that Steinbeck invoked. In any life, we are likely to find it most lively when we are engaged in a creative task that is fresh and risky, especially when that task is all but impossible. Greater challenges draw greater helpers, in and out of the dream worlds.

6. DREAMS ARE A CREATIVE STUDIO

I love kitchen dreams. In my dreams — as often in waking life — the kitchen is a place where good things are mixed together and cooked up. It's the place where my soul, as well as my body, is fed and nourished by a master chef I know to be my inner creator. If my dream kitchen is messy, I pay attention to what I need to sort out in waking life in order to produce something good. If my master chef is unhappy, I jump to take appropriate action. I once cancelled a book contract because I dreamed my master chef — now in the kitchen of an opulent banquet place — did not like my menu and refused to work with it.

To be creative in life does not require us to follow a particular line. You don't need to be a writer, an artist, or a musician to be creative — though you may be in the process of discovering that you are those things, too. To create is to bring something *new* into the world. This requires the willingness to take the risk of going where you have never gone before. To create, you also need to be a "jump thinker," making connections between things most people would never think to connect, whether this is for a novelty party menu, a way of creating more storage space, or a solution for world poverty.

When we go dreaming, we go into a creative studio where we see the prototypes of creative projects of all kinds that we can bring into our physical lives — if we can learn to hold on to those dreams and act on them before they fade away. Aboriginal artists in northern Australia talk about dreams in which they "walk through" the paintings, interacting with the beings and forms they will later paint. By his own account, the stunningly original architect Frank Gehry does something like this in dreams in which he inspects structures that he later designs. Sometimes, in Gehry's dreams, he gets counsel from interesting people. When he was designing a cancer treatment center in Glasgow, a friend who had died from breast cancer told him in a dream that he needed to make the shapes of the building more feminine to reassure and encourage women patients; Gehry proceeded to work in elements that evoke the delicacy and beauty of lace.

As with the "secret laboratory" of science, a creative engagement with dreams is not just a matter of "Eureka!" moments — like the dream that gave Jack Nicklaus a new golf grip, or the dream that gave Beethoven a canon, or the dream in which Italian mathematician Cardan composed a whole book that he was then able to transcribe. Dreaming gives us a creative studio where we can go anytime we like, and from which we can bring fresh insights and renewed energy for the ever-evolving creative project called life.

Still, those great one-night stands of dream creativity are fabulous, so just for fun let's review a few to show how important they have been.

Dream Music

John Lennon said, "The best songs are the ones that come to you in the middle of the night, and you have to get up and write them down, so you can go back to sleep." This has been true for many rock musicians. The music for the Rolling Stones hit "(I Can't Get No) Satisfaction" came to guitarist Keith Richards in a dream in Clearwater, Florida, in 1965. As he stirred from sleep, he grabbed a guitar and turned on a tape recorder so he wouldn't lose the notes he was playing fresh from the dream. He fell back asleep as soon as he had played the notes once, so most of the tape is snoring — but the music remained. Roy Orbison recorded "In Dreams" as soon as he woke from the dream that gave him the song. Pat Monahan, lead singer for Train, woke with a song in his head and immediately recorded a demo of "Drops of Jupiter." Johnny Cash dreamed the arrangement of "Ring of Fire" — with mariachi horns — and got the idea for "The Man Comes Around" from Queen Elizabeth II (in a dream encounter). Paul McCartney woke up with the music for what became the Beatles hit "Yesterday," but the lyrics took some work; for days he was wandering around singing "scrambled eggs."

Bach Teaches a Great Violinist to Dance the Chaconne

Dreams have played a central role in the life of the great contemporary violinist Arnold Steinhardt. The high point of this story, for me, involves an almost unbearably beautiful piece of music.

Bach's Chaconne turns a key in the soul. It gives voice to inconsolable grief. It is achingly lovely; it lays the heart open and frees the spirit, like a bird, to soar on shining wings.

Bach wrote the Chaconne when he returned from a trip with his princely employer to find that his beloved wife, Maria Barbara, had died in his absence and was already buried. He made it the fifth movement of his Partita in D Minor. Less than fifteen minutes in length, the Chaconne is the grail of solo violinists, fiendishly challenging.

Arnold Steinhardt, the first violinist of the Guarneri String Quartet, was asked to play the Chaconne at the funeral of a dear friend, Petra, who had died tragically young. He had played the Chaconne many times before, and recorded a wonderful rendition, but his grief over the loss of his friend drove him to study again how the music *wanted* to be played. He practiced and practiced, using a facsimile of Bach's original music, listened to the recordings of other great violinists, and consulted friends and mentors.

Then he dreamed he was up in the attic of his friend's house, where he used to practice with the skylight open to give space for the strokes of his bow. In his dream, Petra brought Bach up the stairs to meet him.

Bach was not wearing his flowing wig and was dressed in contemporary clothes, but his identity was immediately clear. What good fortune for me! thought Steinhardt. Here was a golden opportunity to get at the Chaconne's essence from the master himself.

Steinhardt opened the skylight to play for Bach, but the composer waved the violin away. Steinhardt tried to ask him about the connection between the music and the death of Bach's wife, but instead of responding, Bach seized his arms and began to dance with him in the cramped attic space. Bach danced slowly, gracefully, guiding the violinist through the steps, while humming the rhythm of the Chaconne. He was teaching Steinhardt to *dance* the Chaconne.

The violinist carried that thrilling sense of movement into his subsequent performances, at his friend's funeral, and later — in a personal tribute to the source of the music — at the grave of Maria Barbara Bach.

Steinhardt's beautiful memoir, *Violin Dreams*, celebrates his passionate, lifelong love affair with the instrument that cries and sings, and he describes how at every turning, his rich dream life has supported his calling. He opens the book with a dream that sends him on a quest to learn the history and prehistory of the violin. In another dream, a beautiful woman visitor reveals herself as the soul of a violin.

Dreams of Writing

Dreams are an incredible gift to writers. For one thing, writing a dream in your journal gets you started. You are immediately working your writing muscles and warming up. A dream can give you the whole story. Jacqueline Mitchard says she dreamed the story of her powerful first novel, *The Deep End of the Ocean*; it then took her several years to bring all of it through. Even a fragment can get your writing fingers working. Three years before his death, Egyptian novelist and Nobel laureate Naguib Mahfouz said that a writer must write something every day. Even if his energy is dwindling, every day a writer must write something, anything. What he did was to write vignettes of his dreams. "They are very, very short stories, like this," he said, pointing to the tip of his index finger.

It's not just that dreams give us creative ideas; they supply creative *energy*. Stephen King recalls that the idea for *Misery* (like the ideas for many of his novels) came to him from a dream, in this case when he was napping on a plane bound for London. He dreamed of a woman who held a writer captive until she eventually killed him, skinned him, fed his remains to a pig — and used a piece of his skin to bind his novel. As soon as King got to Brown's Hotel, he dashed off the first fifty pages of a draft. The plot changed a lot in the telling, but the first vision of the book, and the raw energy for bringing it through, were the gift of the dream.

Robert Louis Stevenson described the central role of dreaming and dreamlike states in his creative process in "A Chapter on Dreams." During his sickly childhood, he was often oppressed by night terrors and the "night hag." But as he grew older, he found that his dreams often became welcome adventures, in which he would travel to far-off places or engage in costume dramas among the Jacobites. He often *read* stories in his dreams, and as he developed the ambition to become a writer, it dawned on him that a clever way to get his material would be to transcribe what he was reading in his sleep. "When he lay down to prepare himself for sleep, he no longer sought amusement, but printable and profitable tales." And his dream producers accommodated him. He noticed they became especially industrious when he was under a tight deadline. When "the bank begins to send letters" his "sleepless Brownies" worked overtime, turning out marketable stories.

"Who are the Little People? They are near connections of the dreamer's, beyond doubt. . . . What shall I say they are but just my Brownies, God bless them! who do one-half my work for me while I am fast asleep, and in all human likelihood, do the rest for me as well, when I am wide awake and fondly suppose I do it for myself. That part which is done while I am sleeping is the Brownies' part beyond contention; but that which is done when I am up and about is by no means necessarily mine, since all goes to show the Brownies have a hand in it even then. . . . My Brownies are somewhat fantastic, like their stories hot and hot, full of passion and the picturesque, alive with animating incident; and they have no prejudice against the supernatural." And have no morals at all.

7. DREAMS HELP US TO MEND
OUR DIVIDED SELVES

"The soul is something that is always trying to leave," announced a sad young woman in one of my workshops — sad until she received the gift of soul recovery, and the light came back on in her eyes and her life.

Most of us know what it feels like to be missing a part of ourselves, or to encounter someone who is "not all there." This is reflected in our everyday speech. We might say of ourselves, "I was out to lunch," or of someone else, "He is a few sandwiches short of a picnic."

Western psychology offers many tools and models for dealing with aspects of the self that are present within an individual. It rarely addresses the problem of what to do when aspects of the self are missing.

Soul loss may be caused by pain or abuse, trauma or heartbreak. We are hurt or scarred so deeply that a part of ourselves leaves the body and does not come back because it does not want to suffer the same grief or trauma again.

Soul loss also results from life choices. We decide to leave a relationship, a home, a job, a country, a lifestyle — and part of us resists that choice, sometimes to the point of splitting away and withdrawing its energy from our lives.

We lose soul when we make the choice to give up on our *big* dreams, when we refuse to make that creative leap of faith, or to trust ourselves to love.

We lose soul when we take up the habit of lying, to ourselves or others.

Our dreams show us how to heal our divided selves and bring missing parts of our energy and identity back into the body, where they belong.

Dream Invitations to Soul Recovery

Here are some of the ways in which dreams introduce soul matters and open paths for soul energy to come home.

Dreams about Shoes

Shoes have "soles" and dreams of shoes often involve "soul" in the deeper sense. In dreams, the state of your shoes — especially if one or more is missing — may be telling you about something that has happened to your soul.

Dreams of the Old Place

Dreams in which we go back to a scene from our earlier lives, especially when this happens over and over, may indicate that a vital part of our energy and identity is still in that old place. We may find ourselves returning in dreams, again and again, to a childhood home, or the home we shared with a former partner. These dreams may be an invitation to reach back into that place and recover one of our soul-selves that is stuck there. The "old place" may also prove to be a place of encounter with family members and loved ones who have passed on — or need help in passing on.

Dreams of Our Younger Self as a Separate Individual

These types of dreams may be nudging us to recognize and recover a part of ourselves we lost at that younger age. Sometimes we do not know who that beautiful child is, until we take a closer look.

Sometimes we see our missing parts in that magic mirror.

Roger dreamed he looked in a mirror and saw many selves, aspects of himself at many different ages. He was thrilled as he watched them coming together, hugging each other, and uniting — all except for a shy five-year-old who drew further and further away.

Roger went back inside the dream — through a technique we call dream reentry — and offered his five-year-old self toys he had loved, coaxing him with thoughts like: "You don't *have* to come over here. But if you want to have some fun . . ." When his five-year-old self finally came back, Roger felt lighter and charged with energy.

Maggie shared a dream in which she recognized a lovely three-year-old who was hiding out in Grandma's yard — and realized, *in the dream*, that it was time to get her lost child out of the old place. "My three-year-old wouldn't come over the fence until I offered her a cute little stuffed lion. Then she came with me. We had a picnic and sang over and over, 'Lock her up and take her home, take her home, take her home.' I know my little girl is with me now."

Animal Helpers Guide Us to Our Missing Selves

Many *big* dreams that offer an invitation to soul recovery involve animal guides.

A woman named Peggy told me a dream in which she was standing on a hillside, surrounded by other figures she slowly began to recognize as aspects of herself — a baby self, a lively teenager, and a sad and estranged eleven-year-old. She wanted to bring the whole group together, but the eleven-year-old turned her back and moved off.

Peggy looked down across the valley and saw an animal feeding in the distance. It raised its head, and she saw it was a large black bear. The force and directness of its gaze were shocking. The bear came racing toward Peggy, climbing the hill at amazing speed. As it neared her, it raised up on its hind legs. Peggy stood frozen before the bear. The bear took her hand in its great paw and told her, "I am your very best friend."

Peggy woke elated, charged with energy, feeling that her life was full of possibility. I shared her joy, because the dream offered so many gifts and such profound and immediate healing. In her dream, Peggy was able to recognize different aspects of herself — including younger selves who had been missing for many years through soul loss — and bring them together. And she acquired a powerful ally. The dream left something important to be re-solved: how to bring home the energy of that eleven-year-old self. Peggy decided to work with the help of her "very best friend," through the dream reentry technique, to bring that eleven-year-old child home.

Sometimes the process of soul recovery and integration may be completed with the help of dream animals inside a single night dream. A woman named Holly dreamed a dog and a fox rescued four younger versions of herself — pieces that had been missing for many years — from a place deep underground. The dream animals brought Holly and her four child selves to a blue lake of healing where they bathed and played together and became one.

The Absence of Dream Recall

A primary symptom of soul loss is the inability to remember one's dreams — as if the part of the sufferer that knows how to dream and travel in deeper reality has gone away, out of pain or disgust. We begin to practice soul recovery for ourselves, and support it in others, when we agree to make a little room each day for our dreams to come back. We start by agreeing that when we wake up, we will recall something from the night — even if it is not a dream. In this way, we signal to our dream source that we are ready to receive.

"Hidden within the grown-up heart," as Rilke sings of those who have been hurt and have hurt others, is "a longing for the first world, the ancient one." In German, that "longing" (*ein Atemholen*) can also be rendered as a "breathing toward." The breath of our longing reaches for the wonder and vitality and innocence of our beautiful lost boys and girls and their "first world" of dreams and enchantment. When we open the dream door, we will find our way to them, and they to us.

8. DREAMING IS A KEY
TO BETTER RELATIONSHIPS

We can dream our way to the partner who fulfills us emotionally, spiritually, and physically. Working with dreams and sharing them in the right way can help us deepen and renew exciting relationships. In dreams, we also learn when it is time to cut our losses and move away from a cramped or destructive relationship.

Gabby dreamed she was with a tall, attractive Jewish man who resembled the TV host of *America's Funniest Home Videos*. Like Bob Saget, the man in her dream was funny and had great theatrical flair. In the dream, Gabby took this man to visit her family in South Korea, introducing him as "the man I'm going to marry." They loved him, too.

Gabby was amazed by this dream — especially by her family's reaction to her intended, since they had long made it clear that they wished her to marry a Korean in a traditional ceremony.

Nine months later, she met the man from her dream — in one of my workshops in Manhattan. Like Bob Saget, Roger is over six feet tall and Jewish, has a great sense of humor, and is both an actor and a playwright. As they got to know each other, Roger realized he had been dreaming of Gabby. Their interweaving dreams grew until they were married on a beach on Long Island in the summer of 2006.

Maybe we would do better with our relationships if we *required* each other to dream on what wants to happen between us.

There is a very illuminating story about this in an Icelandic saga. The king of Denmark wanted to marry a woman named Thyri, the beautiful daughter of the earl of Holstein.

Thyri's father — clearly an enlightened man — informed the king that his daughter must choose for herself, "since she is much wiser than I am."

Thyri told the king that he must build himself a new house, just big enough for a bed, where no house has stood before. He must sleep alone in this place — a dream incubator — for three nights and pay close attention to his dreams. Then he must send a messenger to her with an exact report of what he has dreamed. "If you don't dream," Thyri cautioned the king, "don't bother to call on me again."

The king remembered his dreams, and Thyri must have approved of the content, because she agreed to marry him and became first among his counselors. She is remembered as the wisest queen of Denmark, who helped the king — through her dream tracking — to see the hidden forces behind events and make good choices.

Dreams Show Us How to Move On — or Move Out

Dreams hold up a mirror to our relationships. A Japanese American woman concerned about her marriage dreamed that she and her husband were at the beach. She wanted to plunge in the surf, but he complained that the ocean was "dirty." He took her to a shallow ornamental pool where the water was only a few inches deep and told her it was okay to bathe there. She recognized that this was a fairly exact video clip of her situation; she resolved that she would try find a way to get her husband beyond the formality and shallowness of their marriage — and failing that, move beyond it.

Dreams can also help us renew and regrow a relationship by showing us depths of power and passion in ourselves and our partners that we may now be able to claim. A man who had been getting bored in his marriage dreamed he was making love with a voluptuous goddess whose body seemed to take form from the living Earth, then changed into the shape of his wife. He approached his wife with new eyes, and something like awe. "How come it took you all this time to wake up to the fact you're married to a goddess?" his wife teased him when he finally found the courage to tell her the dream.

Then there are the dreams that show us it's time to move out. A Texan named Ingrid decided to ask for dream guidance on her marriage, which had seemed flat and unfulfilling for quite a while. In her dream, she was at a take-out place with succulent Tex-Mex cuisine, which she loved. She put in her order and paid the cashier, but was kept waiting and waiting while droves of other people came and went, getting their food without delay. A musician she found cute said to her, as he picked up his own dinner, "This place sucks."

She woke from the dream feeling sad and drab. Following a five-minute dream process with me (see chapter 3), she came up with this one-liner: "I'm in a place where I will never be nourished or fed, however long I wait." She asked her husband for a divorce right after this dream. She has since remarried — to a musician who strongly resembles the cute guy in the dream.

Dreams Coach Us on Family Transitions

Dreams coach us in how to handle family transitions. I'll confine myself here to an example that will speak to any parent.

Susan's dream led her to confront the issue of how to provide for her teenage son's safety while allowing him his own room to grow. While the family was preparing for a vacation in Hawaii, Susan dreamed her son went far out in the water with a slightly older boy — then vanished. She was terrified, but knew her son was beyond her reach. She woke desperately troubled. When her son spontaneously decided, not long after, that he did not want to go to Hawaii but would stay with friends, Susan let go of her fear that the dream would be literally fulfilled, and she applied herself to using its guidance in improvisational ways. She carefully explored who would be supervising her son while the family was away, and she made him agree not to ride with a slightly older boy who was a notoriously reckless driver. Susan worked with the more general message of the dream: how can I prepare my son to handle life challenges on his own?

In Dreaming, We Can Heal
Our Relations with the Departed

Dreams help us to heal our relationship with the departed as well as those who share our physical lives. Countless dreamers, every night, experience the fact that in dreams, contact with the "dead" is entirely natural. This can be the source of much-needed forgiveness and closure and of important mutual guidance. In the year after his death, my father appeared to me and another family member repeatedly in dreams — blessedly released from the symptoms of a crippling stroke — sharing love and encouragement and very specific advisories for the well-being of the family.

I am reminded of the following scene: I was giving an informal talk in a bookstore in Simsbury, Connecticut. A lovely elderly man named Bob recounted a dream in which he was visiting a beautiful place on a river. He was received with great affection, but eventually decided it was time to leave. He was told firmly, "No, you can't leave yet." He realized this was because his (departed) wife was there, and he needed to see her. He wanted to bring her food. When he got to her, he saw that she was surrounded by an abundance of everything she could want — the finest foods, books, beautiful flowering gardens. They had a loving reunion. He woke very happy. Now he wanted to know what he should *do* with the dream.

I suggested that if he just relaxed — in light meditation in an easy chair, or in bed before sleeping, he could reenter his dream — and that if it were my dream, I would want to do this as often as possible. Bob came up to me at the end of the talk with shining eyes, very grateful for validation and guidance along his path. He now had an address on the other side, and knew his way.

At the same talk, a woman shared a troubling dream in which her deceased father visited her and — challenged by her — admitted that he had abused her when she was very young. I talked about what Yeats called the "dreaming back" phase of the after-life transition, in which the departed visit the living in the dream-space in search of understanding of what they did (or failed to do) in the life experience that has just ceased. While they may come later for forgiveness, a first step in their progression toward purgation and release may be simply to recognize and admit what their actions and their consequences were, from a clearer perspective. The woman found this very helpful and said she was willing to explore whether she could reach a point where she could forgive her father and extend love and blessing to him.

In a society where we are rarely taught that contact with the departed is natural and that healing and forgiveness are possible beyond the apparent barrier of death — and where few of us are given effective preparation for the journey beyond death — our dreams are our vital mentors.

9. DREAMS RECALL US TO OUR LARGER PURPOSE

Dreams recall us to our personal truth. In life's storms of conflicting agendas, they restore our inner compass. Our conscience speaks to us in dreams to remind us that without truth we are lost.

There is a Persian story about this that I love. The story is about a king who falls into habits of deceit. He lies to himself and to others, and this so disgusts his soul that it takes flight, as a falcon, from his heart, and flies far away. When the king cleans up his act, his soul-bird comes back. When he again succumbs to the way of lies and deceit, the falcon of soul leaves him forever. The king sickens, and the kingdom falls to ruin.

This dreamlike story comes alive — in ways that speak to each of us — in our dreams.

We also learn, in dreams, that the part of ourselves that thinks and chooses in ordinary circumstances is not the wisest part of ourselves, and it may be utterly clueless about what really matters — such as the reason we came into a body in this world in the first place.

I learned from a dream guide in my childhood that the most important knowledge comes to us through *anamnesis*, which means "remembering" the knowledge that belonged to us, on the level of soul and spirit, before we came into this world. Dreaming is the best way I know to practice *soul remembering*. We live differently when we remember that our lives have a purpose, one we consciously accepted before we came here, and that the ups and downs of our present lives are part of a bigger story.

The Workplace as a Sacred Place

Sometimes dreams remind us that the larger story is being played out in the midst of everyday life, in the place where we live or work.

Patrick, a state government employee, dreamed he was standing in front of a bank of elevators on a high floor of the building where he worked. He turned and was amazed to see an elevator door materializing in the opposite wall, where there were no elevators in physical reality. The door opened and he stepped in. The elevator carried him down to ground level. When he got out, he looked up and saw that his workplace had changed. His building had somehow become part of a mountain, and in the face of the mountain was the shape of an immense winged angel. A voice informed Patrick, "This is a sacred place."

Patrick drew immense guidance, both practical and spiritual, from this dream. It taught him that there is really no distance between ordinary reality and the deeper world of meaning. It made him keenly aware that our regular jobs — our engagement with the regular everyday world — can be part of living our sacred purpose. There does not need to be a separation.

Called to the Banquet of Life

Marc Allen, cofounder and publisher of New World Library, recalls that in his twenties, he was "a Zen student who wanted to live like Saint Francis." He thought money would corrupt his soul, and he scrounged to come up with $65 to pay the rent on a slum apartment. More than usually broke and down on his luck as he approached his thirtieth birthday, he decided he would try to come up with an "ideal picture" of what he really wanted to do. To his surprise, he saw that he wanted to create a publishing company that would produce his own and his friends' books and make everyone a comfortable living. He founded that company, with his friend Shakti Gawain, but it was soon in danger of financial collapse. Marc was aware that, in some part of himself, he was blocking his own success.

One night he dreamed he was climbing a mountain. The ascent was very hard at first, over steep and rocky ground. Then he came to a broad path winding round to the right. It brought him to the mouth of a cave, sealed by an iron gate with a "tangle of wrought iron" at the center. As he examined the "tangle" more closely, he found the handle of a sword. When he pulled out the sword, the gate opened at once.

He entered the cave. It was very dark, and as he advanced the space became smaller and tighter, but the sword in his hand gave him the courage to proceed. He came to a light-filled space where three huge banquet tables had been set up.

The first table was piled high with gifts and treasures — miniature houses, gold coins, electronic equipment, musical instruments, lots of expensive "stuff." A voice told Marc: "This is the material plane. There is nothing you need to reject. It is here for your enjoyment and mastery."

On the second table, he saw the four magical implements — the wand and the cup, the sword and the pentacle — familiar to him from tarot. The voice told him: "This is the astral plane of magic. There is nothing to reject here either. It is for your enjoyment and mastery."

The third table appeared to be bare, except for the tablecloth, which shimmered as if it was spun from light. The voice told him: "This is the spiritual plane. It is everywhere, part of everything. It is your essence; you've always been here, and you always will be."

Marc spread his arms, filled with relief and peace, and he floated upward, into the center of the great cathedral-like space, feeling the all-pervasive light permeating every cell of his body.

He woke from his dream, lying on his back, arms spread wide. He was filled with the warmth of the light and with a newfound clarity. The message he received was: *Go for it. Don't hold back.* The dream spurred him to re-vision his business and to plunge forward with more expansive plans and greater dreams. He says that single dream was worth years of therapy, and he credits it with giving him the energy and focus to turn a struggling company into a notable success.

Dreams Put Us in Touch with Inner Teachers

There is a passage in Dante's "Purgatorio" where he encounters his radiant guide in the form of a lovely woman named Beatrice, who reproaches him for not heeding the dreams in which she sought him, over many years. The message is clear and enduring: Our true spiritual teachers are looking for us, which is why they can always be found. They especially come looking for us in dreams, when we move beyond the self-limiting beliefs and consensual hallucinations of the little everyday mind.

The guides who come to us in dreams put on masks or costumes adapted to our level of understanding. There is an old Greek saying that "the gods love to travel in disguise."

The guide may appear with a familiar face — that of an old friend or a departed loved one. The sacred guide may appear in a form that has been shaped by our religious upbringing — or in a form that is wildly shocking to conventional beliefs. Genuine teachers often love to shock us awake.

The most important teacher we'll encounter is no stranger: it is our own Higher Self. Listen to this beautiful account of the arrival of a guide by the great Persian philosopher and visionary traveler Suhrawardi:

> One night I experienced a dreamlike ecstasy. Suddenly I was wrapped in gentleness; there was a blinding flash, then a diaphanous light in the likeness of a human being. There he was: helper of souls, imam of wisdom, whose form filled me with wonder and whose shining beauty dazzled me. He said to me, "Come back to yourself, and your problem will be solved."

Unfinished Portrait of the Higher Self

I dreamed once I was leading a group on a spiraling path, up toward a beautiful towerlike building. Immense carved animals were stationed as guardians of the four quarters; one was a lion with a tremendous carnelian inlaid in its back that flashed fire in the sunlight. Through one of the high, open archways of the building, I gazed in wonder at an unfinished painting. It rose for several stories, at least — higher than I could track. At the very bottom of the painting was a human figure, tiny in comparison to the painting as a whole. It stood like a candle flame. Around it and above it, in light shimmering bands of color, were larger energy forms, growing and going up and up. I knew the name of this painting. In the dream, I had read this in my local paper. The painting was called, "Unfinished Portrait of the Higher Self."

I did not see the artist in the dream, but the clue was in the dream newspaper: this was local news. It was about the dreamer — and also, I suspect, about all dreamers.

In the hurry and clutter of our regular lives, it is easy to lose touch with our larger identity and purpose. Dreams put us back in touch with the Higher Self. They help us to rise to a level of perception from which we can view life's stresses and challenges with some degree of detachment and see how current tests may be part of a larger plan.

Taking Courage from Dreams

In a stirring phrase, Synesius of Cyrene — a fourth-century bishop who wrote the best book on dreams (in my opinion) before the modern era — observed that God makes the dreamer "fruitful with his own courage."

Yes: there are dreams that charge us with courage for a life mission, the courage that comes from remembering and living a bigger story — the kind of courage evoked in *The Return of the King*, the third book of J. R. R. Tolkien's trilogy the *Lord of the Rings*. Whether or not you are a lover of Tolkien, there is a climactic moment in the final book (which comes across powerfully in the movie version) that wonderfully demonstrates the courage and the energy that become available when we claim and act from our larger selves. A monstrous army has grown to unbeatable size. The odds against the forces of good are overwhelming. The battle against darkness can only be won when the true king (Aragorn) stops pretending he is just a borderline figure (a Ranger) and stands in his majesty and power. When he does that, he is able to command legions of the damned to march with him against the greater evil, and the day is won.

EVERYDAY DREAM GAMES

You don't want anyone telling you what your dreams mean. Really, you don't. As we have seen, dreams bring many gifts of power, and you don't want to give that power away by letting someone else tell you what your dream (or your life) means.

What's that? You need help? Your dream is mysterious, and you can't figure it out. Maybe you asked for dream guidance on an issue, and you remembered a dream, but you can't see a connection between the dream content and the question you had in your mind when you put your head on the pillow.

It's okay to ask for help. Personally, I take all the help I can get when exploring my dreams. The kind of person who can help most with a dream is someone who will give you feedback and counsel on action without taking your power away. That person does not have to be an "expert" on dreams or anything else.

Now of course, dream interpreters have been in high demand in many societies. Think of the stories of Daniel and Joseph in the Old Testament. In ancient Mesopotamia (now modern Iraq, alas), the dream interpreter was a powerful figure, often standing very close to the king. In one Mesopotamian text, the dream guide is described as "one who lies at a person's head." This is a very interesting clue that the best dream guides in this culture were doing something very different from verbal analysis. They made it their game to try to enter the dreamer's situation and psychic space — and to speak from that place.

Imagining yourself in someone else's place is part of the game we are about to learn. It need not involve "lying at a person's head" (unless you're already in bed together when you start playing).

After a lifetime of exploring and sharing dreams, I have invented a fun way to share dreams, to get some nonauthoritarian and nonintrusive feedback, and to move toward creative action. I call this the Lightning Dreamwork Game. It's like lightning in two senses — it's very quick (you can do it in five minutes), and it focuses and brings through terrific energy. It's a game you can play just about anywhere, with just about anyone — with the stranger in the line at the supermarket checkout, or with the intimate stranger who shares your bed. The rules are simple, and they open a safe space to share even the most sensitive material.

LIGHTNING DREAMWORK GAME

You can play this game with two or more people. We'll call the principal players the Dreamer and the Partner.

There are four moves in the Lightning Dreamwork Game.

First Move

The Dreamer tells the dream as simply and clearly as possible, as a story. Just the facts of the dream, no background or autobiography. In telling a dream this way, the Dreamer claims the power of the story. The Partner should ask the Dreamer to give the dream report a title, like a story or a movie.

Second Move

The Partner asks the Three Big Questions. (1) How did you feel? (2) Reality check: What do you recognize from this dream in the rest of your life, and could any part of this dream be played out in the future? (3) What do you want to know about this now?

The Dreamer answers all three questions.

Third Move

The Partner now shares whatever thoughts and associations the dream has triggered for him or her. The Partner begins by saying, "If it were my dream, I would think about such-and-such." The etiquette is very important. By saying "if it were my dream," we make it clear that we are not setting out to tell the Dreamer what his or her dream — or life — means. We are not posing as experts of any kind. The Partner is just sharing whatever strikes him or her about the dream, which may include personal memories, other dreams, or things that just pop up. (Those seemingly random pop-ups are often the best.)

Fourth Move

Following the discussion, the Partner asks the Dreamer: What are you going to do now? What action will you take to honor this dream or work with its guidance? If the Dreamer is clueless about what action to take, the Partner will offer his or her own suggestions, which may range from calling the guy up or buying the pink shoes to doing historical or linguistic research to decode odd references. Or, the Dreamer may want to go back inside the dream (see below) to get more information or move beyond a fear. One thing we can do with any dream is to write a personal motto, like a bumper sticker or something that could go on a refrigerator magnet.

Lightning Dreamwork is suitable for almost any group environment. A company manager who had taken one of my trainings introduced her department to the Lightning Dreamwork Game. They found it so much fun — and so helpful in bringing through specific guidance — that the members of her office agreed to devote twenty minutes each morning to sharing dreams as a group. Instead of a diversion of time and energy, the game was highly energizing and became the source of creative business solutions as well as personal healing.

GOING BACK INSIDE YOUR DREAMS

The best way to get to the meaning of a dream is to go back inside the dream and reclaim more of the full experience. The dream experience should not be confused with the remembered dream, which is often blurry or fragmentary. Going back inside a dream will tell us whether the dream images should be regarded literally, symbolically, or as glimpses of a separate reality into which we have traveled during the night.

We may want to go back inside a dream to gather more information. For example, a friend who was a senior executive at a Fortune 500 corporation dreamed he was summoned to a beach house during a work crisis in which he was in danger of losing his job. He did not recognize the dream location, though he speculated that the beach house could be the second home of one of his bosses. I suggested that he might want to reenter the dream and get some more information. I assisted him by helping to clarify his intention — *I will revisit the beach house and find out about the work crisis* — and by giving him some fuel for the journey, in this case the steady beat of a frame drum.

In a relaxed posture, with his eyes covered, following the beat of the drum, my friend was able to revisit the dream house exactly as he might have gone back to a house he had visited in ordinary reality. He learned that it was indeed the second home of one of his bosses, and he acquired specific details about the crisis in the offing that could cost him his job. As a result of this dream re-entry, my friend accomplished two things. First, he was able to use the early warning of a work crisis to take appropriate steps to safeguard his job. Second, when the crisis he had previewed did erupt, and he was summoned to an emergency meeting at the beach house he had visited in his dream, he was on the right side of the table — and did not need to ask directions to the restroom.

Another good reason to go back inside a dream is to move beyond a fear. Suppose you dream that there is an intruder in your house. Surely you would want to know whether this is a literal intruder — in which case you would need to ensure your physical security — or a symbolic intruder, perhaps a disease that could break into your body. Or, is the intruder actually an aspect of your bigger Self, before whom the little everyday self often cowers in fear? One way of knowing would be to step back inside the dream-space and check out the intruder on the ground where he appeared.

Other reasons to go back inside a dream? To have a proper conversation with someone who showed up during the night, perhaps a departed loved one, a personal mentor, or a spiritual guide. Or, perhaps the dream was simply fun. You were having a wonderful time in Paris, or Hawaii, or another star system, and you were pulled out by the alarm clock or your kid jumping on the bed, and you would like more of the dream.

How do we get back into a dream?

In my workshops and private consultations, as in the case of the friend who was summoned to the beach house, I follow a simple dream reentry technique. As explained below, I like to use steady heartbeat drumming to help the dreamer relax and shift consciousness and flow back inside the dream. The effect of the drumming is to shepherd brainwaves into the rhythms associated with hypnagogic states and sometimes REM sleep. It minimizes the clutter of distracting thoughts. And it works like jet fuel in powering the journey. For private use at home, I recommend using a drumming CD.

The Dream Reentry Technique

Going back into a dream is like going back to any place you have visited. It is the same as imagining yourself returning to a friend's house or to a landscape you visited on vacation.

To prepare for a dream reentry, do the following:

1. Pick a Dream with Real Energy.

As long as it has juice, it doesn't matter whether the dream you want to reenter is from last night or twenty years ago. It can be a tiny fragment or a complex narrative. You can choose to work with a night dream, a vision, or a waking image. What's important is that the dream you choose to revisit has some charge — whether it is exciting, seductive, or challenging.

2. Relax.

Follow the flow of your breathing, and relax. If you are holding tension in any part of your body, tense and relax those muscle groups until you feel yourself becoming loose and comfy.

3. Focus on a Specific Scene from Your Dream.

Let a specific scene from your dream become vivid on your mental screen. Let all your senses become engaged, until you can touch it, smell it, hear it, and taste it.

4. Clarify Your Intention.

Before you begin, come up with clear and simple answers to these two questions: (1) What do you want to know? (2) What do you intend to do, once you are back inside the dream? Remember these intentions as you reenter the dream.

5. Call in Guidance and Protection.

As you begin, or at any time, you may choose to invoke a sacred guardian by a familiar name, or you can simply ask for help in the name of Love and Light.

6. Give Yourself Fuel for the Journey.

Heartbeat shamanic drumming works well for many people and most groups. If live drumming is not possible, you may want to use my shamanic drumming CD for dream travelers, *Wings for the Journey*.

HELPING CHILDREN WITH DREAMS

Adults are not the only ones who need help understanding their dreams. Kids do too. And they need the same kind of sympathetic, respectful feedback that is asked for in the Lightning Dreamwork Game above. One of the very worst things to say to a child is "It's only a dream." To kids, dreams are real. Trying to convince them otherwise is experienced as a form of abandonment.

When it comes to their dreams, our kids need just three things from us.

Full Attention and Close Listening

Children need us to listen to them — really listen, which means no cell phones and no interruptions — for the few minutes required to tell a dream. Ask questions that help the child draw out and remember the dream, but resist the urge to interpret or analyze the dream for them. This is something children do *not* need. When we give children our undivided attention as they tell a dream, we are helping them to claim their voices and become storytellers and communicators. We offer them a safe way to surface issues that may need to be addressed within the family. We also allow them to teach us about the dream world, with which kids — especially young kids — are often far more familiar than most adults, who often are out of touch with the dreamer in their own psyches.

A Quick Way to Deal with Scary Stuff

When a child is disturbed by "bad dreams" or nightmares, it's important to try to discern whether the troubling experience was actually a dream or the effect of unsettled psychic energies, either in the home, at school, or elsewhere. Kids pick up disagreements and emotional trouble in the environment, and we need to give them a quick way to get rid of the residue. We can take them outside — or send them into the bathroom — to literally *spit it out*. Or get them to draw a picture of what disturbed them and tear it up. If the bad stuff was going on inside a dream, we want to give the child a guardian who can go with them into the dreamspace. I have often suggested to young children that a favorite stuffed animal, or a toy soldier, represents a dream guardian who will guard them in scary situations in their dreams. This tactic works amazingly well.

A Creative Way to Honor Dreams

Kids love to be invited to do something creative from a dream — turn it into a story, a performance, a drawing, or a painting.

CHAPTER 4

DREAMS ARE a SECRET ENGINE of HISTORY

D reams play a vastly more important role in shaping world events than is acknowledged by most historians (or our media), who are as coy when it comes to reporting dreams as they once were — in times long past — about reporting sex.

A case in point: Sir Martin Gilbert devoted decades of his industrious and scholarly life to producing a magnificent narrative biography of Winston Churchill. Dip into it if you need any reminding that the big events of the first half of the twentieth century — and most notably the defeat of Hitler — are inconceivable without Churchill in a leading role. His prescience, his courage, his extraordinary ability to awaken and mobilize the energies of a whole people got Britain, and the democracies, through their darkest hour.

Now, suppose that Churchill had died before becoming prime minister, say in June 1914, on the eve of the First World War. If you read Gilbert's biography, you'll see that it was entirely possible — indeed probable — that the young Churchill, literally a highflier, could have gotten himself killed during one of his many flying lessons and joyrides around that time. He was a great proponent of early military aviation, when the generals could not see the point. When he became first lord of the admiralty — the ruler of the Royal Navy — he asked the dashing young naval pilots at Eastchurch on the Isle of Sheppey to teach him to fly. They were delighted to oblige. He loved the sense of freedom that came to him at the controls of a seaplane (a word he coined) swooping over the shore. But the risks were amazing. Early planes were flimsy and unstable and constantly cutting out or cracking up in midair. Those who kept count calculated that there was one death for every five thousand flights. Two of Churchill's favorite flight instructors died within days of going up with him, on the same planes they had flown with Winston. Churchill's friends and family, especially his wife, Clementine, begged him to give it up. He refused. He never lacked for courage, and he believed in his own luck.

Then something happened to change his mind. On June 6, 1914, Churchill sent a telegram to his beloved "Clemmie," who was with their young children at her mother's home in Dieppe. He told her he would give up flying at least until their "kitten" was born. (She was pregnant with their third child.) He would do this with regret, since he so loved the air and was so close to earning his pilot's wings. But he would do it all the same.

Churchill's biographer, Martin Gilbert, gives us the text of his telegram to his wife, and we get the hint that Churchill's decision to stop buzzing around in those early flying caskets may well have saved his life. But in the thousand-plus pages of *Churchill: A Life*, Gilbert does not tell us what Clementine said in a telegram she sent to her husband from Dieppe the previous day. In it, she reported on one of her dreams, and this inspired Churchill's decision to give up flying.

Let's restore this world-changing dream to history.

Clementine's telegram to Winston on June 5, 1914, contained the following passage:

> Dearest I cannot help knowing you are going to fly as you go to Sheerness & it fills me with anxiety. I know nothing will stop you from doing it so I will not weary you with tedious entreaties, but don't forget that I am thinking about it all the time & so, do it as little, & as moderately as you can.

Clemmie had sent Winston many previous messages about her fear of his flying. But in this particular message, she told him something more. She told him a terrible dream. It was not a "crash-and-burn" dream, but it was a dream that evidently shook him to the core. Clemmie dreamed she gave birth to an idiot baby, a baby she wanted to kill. Let's look at her own words, with her own punctuation:

> I dreamt that I had my Baby, but the Doctor & Nurse wouldn't shew it to me & hid it away — Finally after all my entreaties had been refused and I jumped out of bed & ran all over the house searching for it. At last I found it in a darkened room. It looked all right & I feverishly undressed it and counted its fingers & toes — It seemed quite normal and I ran out of the room with it in my arms —
>
> And then in the Daylight I saw it was a gaping idiot. And then the worst thing of all happened — I wanted the Doctor to kill it — but he was shocked & took it away from me & I was mad too. And then I woke up & went to sleep again and *dreamt it* a second time. I feel very nervous and unhappy & the little thing has been fluttering all the morning.
>
> Your telegram arrived late last night after we were in

bed — Every time I see a telegram now, I think it is to
announce that you have been killed flying — I had a
fright but went to bed relieved & reassured; but this
morning after the nightmare I looked at it again for con-
solation & found to my horror that it was from Sheerness
& not from Dover where I thought you were going first
— So you are probably at it again at this very moment.

Goodby Dear but Cruel One

Your loving Clemmie

All the Sun is gone to-day

& it has turned very cold & Bleak.

As Churchill himself might have put it, Clementine's dream,
and the fact that she was able to get it through to her husband,
turned the "hinge of fate." Though Winston had ignored all previous appeals from his wife and others to give up flying, this message turned a key inside him. He immediately responded with the
telegram promising her that he would give up flying at least until
their third child was born.

It is instructive to compare the admonitory dream of Churchill's
wife with the warnings received in dreams by the wives of other
great men. Famously, Calpurnia dreamed twice of Caesar's murder the night before he was assassinated. Her dreams were explicit, and yet Julius Caesar ignored them.

Perhaps the indirectness of Clementine's dream was a key to
its reception. Did Winston ask himself whether *he* might be the
"idiot" in question? Did the dream alert him to the possibility that
Clemmie's fears and emotions could endanger her pregnancy?
These questions can't be answered by the surviving documents.
What we do know is that *this* dream persuaded a man who once
said he preferred facts to dreams to accept a dream as a fact. This
may have changed the world, but it is part of the history we are
not taught.

MISSING THE DREAM DIMENSIONS OF ISLAM

It's bad enough that, in the West, we are so often blind and deaf to the role of dreams (and other imaginal events) in our own history. It's even worse that we fail to appreciate their role in societies where dreams and visions are honored and revered. This is one of the critical reasons why the Western democracies have failed to understand — and respond in appropriate ways — to events in the world of Islam that have come to challenge everyone's freedom and security.

All major branches of Islam place a very high valuation on dreaming. This is reflected in the well-known statement (in a hadith attributed to the Prophet Muhammad) that "dreaming is one-forty-sixth part of prophecy." Now, one-forty-sixth of something may not sound like a big deal, but only because we do not understand the context. *All* Muhammad did for the six months prior to the *lailat al-miraj*, the heavenly journey from which he returned with the content of the Koran, was to dream. That journey made him the Prophet. He lived for twenty-three years after that tremendous night of revelation. Six months is one-forty-sixth of twenty-three. In this context to say that dreaming is "one-forty-sixth part of prophecy" is to say it is of the most fundamental importance; it is the key and precondition for prophecy.

Islamic dream psychology distinguishes the *al-ruya*, or "true dream," which may be experienced in sleep or in a waking state of vision. The condition for "true dreaming" is that the dreamer must be in an appropriate state of consciousness, perceiving with the guidance of spiritual allies.

Central to Islamic dream psychology is the belief that in dreams a part of the soul or spirit of the dreamer travels beyond the body and may visit locations at a distance or other dimensions of reality. Through these soul journeys, the dreamer may bring back accurate information about future events or situations at a distance, or may have access to mentors on another plane of reality.

In all major branches of Islam, it is recognized that there is ongoing communication between the dead and the living in dreams. The ninth-century *Book of Dreams* of Ibn Abi al-Dunya includes three hundred vivid accounts of dreams of the dead, including stories of pacts between friends that whoever died first would visit the other and give him a tour of conditions on the other side. Ibn Sirin, the eighth-century author of *Dreams and Their Interpretation* — still the most popular dream book in the Muslim world — pronounced that "Whatever the deceased tells you in sleep is true, for he stays in the world of truth."

Islamic dream psychology is not merely a matter of interpretation. Many Islamic schools teach and practice the skills of transferring consciousness to another realm of reality, a "dream world" believed to be more real, not less real, than the realm of the senses.

The Dream Mandate

Across history, in all major branches of Islam, dreams have been mandates for authority. Leaders have been inspired and then accredited because of powerful dreams, especially dreams involving a personal encounter with the Prophet Muhammad.

The Ottoman Empire, which became an Islamic superpower that dominated the Middle East and southern Europe, traced its origins to the dreams of Osman (1258–1326), the founder of the dynasty. The Ottoman sultan was also the caliph, the "successor" to the Prophet, commander of the faithful, and titular leader of the entire world of Islam.

One of Osman's *big* dreams was a dream of religious conversion. He had come from a fierce tribe of horse warriors who worshipped the powers of sky and earth. On the night a pious Muslim started instructing him in the Koran, an angel appeared to him in a dream and told him that because he honored the Book, his house would be honored from generation to generation. This dream helped to justify the Ottoman caliphate.

In another big dream, Osman saw a great tree grow from his loins until it shadowed the earth. Then he saw the world-city, Constantinople, as a diamond set between sapphires and emeralds in a wedding ring he reached to place on his finger. This dream prophesied world empire and the fall of Constantinople to Osman's descendants in 1453. It also convinced a neighboring Muslim sheikh who had been unimpressed by Osman's pursuit of his beautiful daughter to give him the girl in marriage. The dreamer became Sultan Osman I, and that tree grew for many centuries.

Today, dreams still provide a mandate for political and religious authority in the Islamic world — and sometimes produce an extraordinary mobilizing force to embody the dream — in ways we urgently need to understand.

Look at the career of Mullah Omar, the founder of the Taliban in Afghanistan. He was a physically unimposing, uncharismatic figure. Yet he gathered a devoted and fanatical following at amazing speed as word spread that he had had a true dream, an *al-ruya*, in which the Prophet had charged him with the mission of leading a revolution in his country and transforming the practice of Islam. Mullah Omar's personal dreams very quickly became *movement* dreams, collective dreams.

For Mullah Omar, as for other Islamist leaders — including the leadership of al-Qaeda — dreaming is also valued as a source of secret intelligence. Mullah Omar called the BBC correspondent in Peshawar to discuss a dream in which his brother had seen the White House on fire prior to the September 11 terrorist attacks in 2001. The Taliban leader wanted to check whether details of the White House in his brother's dream were accurate, perhaps in order to gauge its reliability as tactical intelligence. As Taliban leader, Mullah Omar reportedly refused to authorize any military operation unless his dreams sanctioned it.

While Western governments and media may have a hard time accepting that in dreaming we can scout across time and space and gather crucial information, in the Islamic world this is common knowledge. And it is *used*.

I'll give two more examples. One involves a secret factor — a dream factor — in the outcome of a great battle between the Ottomans and the European powers. The other concerns the secret background — the dream background — to the 9/11 terrorist attacks.

The Sultan and the Dream Master

Suleiman the Magnificent (1494–1566), sultan of the Ottoman Empire and caliph of Islam, was the master of many battles. But his luck turned and his army stalled on a campaign in Carinthia. For once, his willpower seemed to fail him. This victor of many battles — and master of three hundred concubines — hesitated in his tent.

Then Suleiman was told that an apprentice of Hudai Effendi was in his camp. Hudai was a sheikh who had accompanied Suleiman in his conquest of the island of Rhodes, and he had been granted a strong hilltop position where he founded a monastery for his order of dervishes. He was known as a master of dreams. He had an enormous bed constructed, big enough to accommodate a dozen dervishes stretched out in all directions. At night, the dream master lay down with twelve of his chosen apprentices, heads together, bodies extended like the spokes of a wheel. They entered *al-ruya* — the state of the true dream — together. They traveled across time as easily as you might walk across a street. The master's great gifts were multiplied to the twelfth power by the cartwheel of dreamers.

Suleiman summoned the apprentice to his tent and told him he had need of the master's sight. He offered him money and safe conduct to travel to Rhodes and return with his sheikh. The dervish surprised the sultan by telling him Hudai Effendi was not far away at all; he promised that the dream master would visit Suleiman before morning prayers. He offered the sultan a "soporific apple" to carry him gently into sleep; Suleiman peeled it and ate it. Before he retired, the sultan told his court officers to stand vigil, and usher Hudai Effendi into his presence as soon as he arrived.

Come morning, the Grand Eunuch was red-eyed and weary with watching. He was certain enough of Suleiman's love to complain that the apprentice was clearly a fraud. "You are wrong," Suleiman responded. "The master visited me in the night and told me he has taken care of everything. He has gone in person to the battlefield and our victory is now certain. A messenger will bring news of it within the hour."

The messenger galloped up punctually, to report that the enemy commander — a prince of Hungary — had been seized by a strange mania and issued crazy and confusing orders to his generals, dooming his side to defeat, before falling from his horse in a dead swoon.

This episode gives us a window into a society in which scouting and psychic operations conducted inside the dream state are a part of high strategy.

Dreams of Terror

Let's move uncomfortably close to the present. One of the most chilling pieces of information to surface after 9/11 was that al-Qaeda operatives and other Islamist extremists were dreaming the details of the terror attacks ahead of time

The source for this statement is a captured videotape, made in

Kandahar on November 5, 2001, that records a conversation between Osama bin Laden and an extremist Saudi cleric about the background to 9/11. They share stories about members of both their networks who were having explicit dreams about the operation prior to the attacks, even though (on the ordinary level) they knew nothing about what was being planned. Many of the sheikh's followers dreamed of planes being flown into tall buildings in America, though they had been told nothing of the hijack plan.

Bin Laden told the sheikh that he became worried that if loose talk about these dreams continued, it could jeopardize operational security. "I was worried that maybe the secret would be revealed if everyone starts seeing it in their dream," he said. So he told one dreamer in his camp who had seen an attack on a tall building in America, "If you see another dream, don't tell anybody."

This bin Laden videotape received extensive play in the media, but the discussion of dreams was generally ignored and received no headlines in the mainstream press, even though it occupied half the transcript and — for the terrorist chief and his interlocutor — was the heart of the matter.

Dreams of a paradise of martyrs and dream visitations from suicide killers who have died have been a major factor in the recruitment and motivation of subsequent al-Qaeda fighters, according to the movement's own propaganda videos. A Saudi member of al-Qaeda who died in Iraq reported three dreams of "black-eyed women in paradise" that made him "passionate" to enter the afterlife. A Yemeni car-bomber who killed himself in an attack on an American military post in Iraq appeared in a comrade's dreams after his death, urging him to "come and join me in paradise." He had made a pact with fellow jihadists prior to his death, promising to visit them from the other side. Such appointments for a dream visitation by the dead have a long pedigree in the history of Islam.

It has been reported that the daily practice of al-Qaeda leaders prior to 9/11 was to share dreams after dawn prayers. How many Western leaders do anything comparable? We are now able to gauge how much they are missing by *not* making room for dreams.

DREAMS SHOW US HUMANITY'S PATH

It may be that just as babies rehearse for walking and talking in dreams before they have developed the corresponding physical abilities, humanity rehearses for new phases in its development through dreaming. We are on the edge of grasping what this might mean when we talk about ideas that are "in the air." We see one facet of it when we learn that artists and science fiction writers have frequently anticipated new technologies by decades or centuries.

Dreaming takes us to a spiritual depth of understanding of our contemporary challenges. It shows us the consequences of present actions and policies, on every scale from individual to planetary. Through dreaming, we can enter the mindset and circumstances of people who are profoundly different and see through their eyes. This can give us the ability to move beyond entrenched prejudice and obsessions about enemies.

As we become *active* dreamers, and share the gifts of dreaming with others, we help to weave webs of peace and healing for our world. The need is very urgent.

I think of the "dream webs" of the Andaman islanders, who got out of the way of the terrible tsunami of December 2004 because their dreams and their intimate connection with the animals and the earth told them it was coming. The Indian government, finding the islanders' coastal fishing camps deserted after the storm, thought they must all have perished. When the Indian government sent reconnaissance helicopters over the highlands, islanders reappeared, shooting arrows at the choppers to indicate that help from New Delhi was *not* wanted or needed. By tradition, the fierce Andaman islanders are group dreamers who gather at night in their community "big houses" to dream the means of survival and progress for the whole community. They picture themselves weaving a dream web across which their dream scouts can move rapidly to gather and bring back information vital to the common interests of the group.

Dreaming expands our options and our sense of possibility as members of the human condition.

A Polish woman told me that during the long years of Soviet dominance and oppression in her country, her dreams were her "films of freedom," encouraging her to believe that she and her people could enjoy a better life.

Our dreams help us to step outside the boxes we put ourselves in or allow others to build around us.

I once dreamed I was strolling around a zoo and became disgusted by the behavior of a crowd of people who were gawping and poking fun at a maned lion through the bars of his cage. Suddenly one of the tourists screamed, "The gate is open!" All the people fled the scene, terrified the lion would get out and attack them. I stepped through the open gate, and the lion jumped up, put his paws on my shoulders, and licked my face like a friendly dog. He wanted me to turn around in order to understand the true situation. When I turned around, I noticed that in this scene it was the *humans*, not the animals, who were living behind bars. The place of the lion was a place of nature, freedom, and unbounded horizons. The lion instructed me in his gravelly lion voice, "You see, humans are the only animals that *choose* to live in cages."

In one way or another, according to our understanding, dreams take us to the place of the lion, the place of freedom. These "films of freedom" not only mentor us on what is possible for us as individuals; they can help to liberate whole communities.

Harriet Tubman's story is a remarkable example. As a young girl in tidewater Maryland, she was badly hurt when an angry overseer threw a two-pound lead weight that hit her in the forehead. This terrible incident seems to have helped open her "third eye." In dreams and visions, she saw herself flying over farmlands and rivers she had never seen with ordinary sight. When dream allies encouraged her to make her break for freedom, she was able to take the aerial pictures from her dreams and use them as maps to get herself safely to freedom. She was inspired by later dreams to return to the South to help others escape to liberty, and again her dreams gave her specific guidance on the roads and river fords and safe houses to use. As the most celebrated conductor of the Underground Railroad, she got three hundred escaping slaves to freedom, never losing one to the posses — because she trusted and worked with her "films of freedom."

The great French observer of the patterns of change and the requirements for political freedom, Alexis de Tocqueville, made this observation in *Democracy in America*: "In times when passions are beginning to take charge of the conduct of human affairs, one should pay less attention to what men of experience and common sense are thinking than to what is preoccupying the imagination of dreamers." Paying attention to "the imagination of dreamers" requires us to track what is developing in the collective mind and in the group mind of specific movements and communities that may produce new events. We need to know what is (or is not) in the vision of leaders and potential world changers. And we want to work for the cause of humanity through our own active dreaming and active imagination.

ONLY
COINCIDENCE

For all that meets the bodily sense I deem
Symbolical, one mighty alphabet
For infant minds, and we in this low world
Placed with our backs to bright Reality
That we may learn with young unwounded ken
The substance from the shadow.

— SAMUEL TAYLOR COLERIDGE,
"THE DESTINY OF NATIONS"

WHERE MIND and MATTER MEET

When do you say, "What a coincidence"?

You think of someone, and they call you on the phone a minute later.

You dream of a bear, and a black bear walks out in front of you on the country road you're driving on.

You are wondering how to get through a harrowing phase of your life, and you look out your car window and see a sign in front of a church that says, COURAGE IS FEAR CONQUERED BY LOVE — and *know* this is for you.

You are remembering, with deep emotion, a time when you wore a beautiful pink dress — and you walk into a boutique where the theme (written in pink lipstick on a mirror) is FANCY GIRLS DREAM IN PINK.

In my personal lexicon, a coincidence is a meaningful convergence of inner and outer experiences. The sense of meaning comes from the observer. That sense may be so strong it is *thrilling*.

Coincidence may be wildly funny. A guy wondering how to handle a date noticed the following bumper sticker on a red sports car in front of him: "Your body is a temple. Mine is an adventure theme park."

Coincidence can inspire a sense of awe, a feeling we are in the presence of the numinous. I was standing in a very clean park — no litter to be seen — talking on my cell phone about how in the Middle Ages the Christ energy came to be identified with the stag. (Yep, that's the kind of conversation I have on the phone, if that's where my head is.) And I glanced down and right at my feet was a round piece of cardboard that might have been a coaster. It displayed a stag with immense antlers with the Calvary cross between them. I have yet to find out who produced this disk — presumably a religious sodality — but I had that unmistakable sense of something reaching through the curtain of the obvious world to give me the message, *Right on*.

I think it's like this: When we go dreaming, we go beyond the curtain of consensus reality. We get out there. We operate outside the rules of a three-dimensional reality, in a spacious Now. We enter parallel and other worlds. Conversely, when coincidence is in play, the powers of that deeper universe — let's call it the multiverse, as scientists often do — come pushing or poking or tickling through the curtain of the obvious to wake us up to the moreness of *everything*.

THINGS THAT FALL TOGETHER

The great psychologist Carl Jung *lived* by coincidence. He achieved a profound understanding that through the study of coincidence we will come to grasp that there is no real separation between mind and matter at any level of reality — a finding confirmed by the best of our physicists. He taught that the incidents of our lives and the patterns of our world are connected by *meaning*, and that meaningful coincidence may guide us to the hidden order of events.

Jung was so fed up with the reflexive dismissal of coincidence as *only* coincidence that he labored heroically to give us a new vocabulary with which to describe both the phenomenon and its character. He coined the word *synchronicity* and defined it as "an acausal connecting principle." These may not quite be household terms, but they have achieved wide circulation, not only within Jungian circles.

The problem is they are not really satisfactory, for reasons Pauli noted with razor-sharp acuity in his extensive correspondence with Jung while the psychologist was working on early drafts of his famous paper on "Synchronicity."

If you go to its Greek origins, *synchronicity* refers to incidents that are *simultaneous*: syn + chron, or happening at the same time. But the most interesting couplings or clusters of coincidence are not necessarily simultaneous. They are patterns of inner and outer events that often play out over time. We may notice a ripple effect of apparent connection over days, weeks, or even years. Jung himself cited a dream, followed by a later waking event that resembled it, as one of the most important instances of "synchronicity," but this is plainly not an example of a simultaneous pairing. Pauli suggested the word *isomorphy* as an alternative to *synchronicity*. He dreamed that a mathematician told him, "We need to build cathedrals to isomorphy." An isomorphy, in this application, would be a pairing or clustering of similar shapes or structures, reappearing in different objects and events. The stress would be on the resemblance of shape, rather than on contiguity in time. It's an attractive idea, but I doubt that *isomorphy* will ever be catchy enough to become an everyday term.

Pauli also liked the old word *correspondence* (as in "meaningful correspondences"), as poets and mystics have always done.

"As above, so below" runs the famous hermetic motto. Things here "correspond" to things above (or below). In the world around us, things also resemble and "correspond" with each other.

Personally, I see no need to give up on the word *coincidence* just because we have fallen into a bad habit of dissing it; habits can be changed.

In its root meaning (from the Latin), a coincidence takes place when two or more incidents "fall together." The word does not specify that these events happen at exactly the same time. But the events are related.

Think of what happens when you toss a set of pick-up sticks. Slow down the motion in your mind's eye, and imagine the sticks coming down very slowly, over an extended period of time. Now imagine a minuscule being who experiences long gaps between the arrival of objects that seem to be falling from thin air and who cannot see where they are coming from. When the observer sees two or more of these objects arrive at the same time, he is amazed and says, "What a coincidence!" When he travels a great distance and finds an object resembling the ones he has just seen, his surprise deepens. When similar objects continue to appear, over variable time intervals, he is astounded. From where he stands, the fall of each stick (or clumping of sticks) is an independent occurrence. It resembles something that happens before or after, but is not causally connected in any way that he can see. He does not know what the game player (a giant invisible to him) knows: events that manifest at discrete points in space and time, as experienced by the minuscule observer, are the result of a single movement on another plane.

Grasp this, and you are on the edge of grasping a very big secret about time. We'll return to this, in time.

I want to reclaim the word *coincidence* because I like the notion of things "falling together" with the implied action of a hidden hand. Coincidences are homing beacons. They are secret handshakes from the universe. They are extraordinary sources of guidance and direction.

We are going to count the ways.

Let's pause for just a moment to note that the idea that co-incidences are important is troubling to some in the psychiatric community. Determined not to be overawed by Jung's learned borrowings from Greek, a Swiss psychiatrst named Klaus Conrad made up the word *apophenia* to describe a psychotic condition he defined as the "unmotivated seeing of connections" accompanied by a "specific experience of an abnormal meaningfulness."

Conrad's Greek was not as good as Jung's. The word he wanted is *apophrenia*, which means "away from the mind." But he left out the "r" in the Greek stem (*phren*), so his coinage — meant to categorize a kind of nonsense — is itself nonsense. The mislabeled condition (mentioned in the title of a rock song and in William Gibson's novel *Pattern Recognition*) is a disorder of com-pulsive pattern recognition that produces paranoid fantasies.

There are people who find meaning and inspiration in the cracks on a wall, and people who are simply cracked. The differ-ence between them may be as extreme as that between Leonardo da Vinci (who urged his apprentices to study cracks in the walls) and the nut portrayed by Mel Gibson in *Conspiracy Theory*. When we navigate by coincidence, we move effortlessly into creative flow. When we project our delusions onto the world around us, we put ourselves in a place of blockage and pain. It is the release or constriction of creative flow that will tell us whether we are on the right track (though let's note that the release may involve a nec-essary redirection of flow).

CAUSATION IN THE MULTIVERSE

Jung described the pairing or clustering of events through mean-ingful coincidence as an "acausal" phenomenon. This raises another problem. Certainly, we do not observe causation in the play of co-incidence in the way that we can say the kettle boiled because we turned on the burner. A characteristic of coincidence is that it does not have a visible cause.

But this does not mean that there is no cause for coincidence. We've already seen — on and off airplanes — some examples of coincidences that feel like they came about because of a hidden agency, or a strong intention, or a trickster or gamester at play just behind the curtain of the obvious world.

Most human cultures, across most of recorded history, have believed that there is indeed a hidden hand at work in coincidence: that it is through the play of unusual or unexpected conjunctions, and natural phenomena, that gods or angels or animate forces of nature or other dimensions send messages to humans or actively intervene in our world. Let's not shrug this off as a "primitive" idea — it has worked, and continues to work, in highly practical ways. And let's not classify this idea as a "metaphysical" belief.

The forces that cause meaningful coincidence may be quite physical. We miss this because we cannot observe their workings with our ordinary senses and our regular assumptions. These forces include our own thoughts and feelings, and those of others connected to us. They may include the powers that Jung called "archetypes" — as long as we remember that in Jung's mature thought the archetypes are not structures but "habitual currents of psychic energy" and "systems of readiness for action," and that they are as much physical as psychic. The physical forces that play with us through coincidence may include our parallel selves in parallel universes, interacting with our world in constant and complex weavings through what quantum physics has taught us to call "interference" patterns, forever shifting the balance of probabilities for any specific outcome.

Quantum physics shows us the universe as a dynamic web of

connection. Subatomic particles are not separate "things"; they have meaning and identity only through their connections with everything else. Those connections do not depend on physical proximity or causation. Particles that have once been in contact with each other remain connected through all space and time.

Quantum physics also confirms that when we go to the heart of physical reality, there is no separation between mind and matter. Subatomic particles exist in all possible states until they are observed — at which point something definite emerges from the soup of possibilities.

Inner and outer, subjective and objective, interweave and move together at quantum levels, on a human scale, and no doubt everywhere in the universe. We live in an energy field where everything resonates — to a greater or lesser degree — with everything else. The world we inhabit mirrors our thoughts and feelings, and vice versa.

In the hidden order of reality, there is no distinction between mind and matter. The split between inner and outer — subjective and objective — that we experience in ordinary life is unknown in the deeper reality.

Richard Wilhelm's account of the Chinese rainmaker contains the essence of a worldview in which the human mind and the external world form a whole. A village has been without rain for weeks. The desperate villagers send for a rainmaker. When the old man arrives, he shuts himself up in the house provided for him, performing no ceremonies until the rains come. When asked how he brought the rain, he explains that when he arrived he noted a state of disharmony in himself, so he retired to compose himself. When he restored his own equilibrium, the rain came according to its natural pattern.

As we become more awake to what is going on, we may become personal magnets for coincidence, "strange attractors" that draw more and more interesting and unexpected encounters and events toward us. The brilliant analyst and classicist Marie-Louise von Franz, who knew both Jung and Pauli well, alluded to this: "The larger our consciousness is, and the more it develops, the more we get hold of certain aspects of the spirit of the unconscious, draw it into our own subjective sphere, and then call it our own psychic activity or our own spirit."

The NINE RULES
of COINCIDENCE

Coincidence may be wild, but it's never truly random. The play of coincidence follows certain rules, and by learning those rules we greatly improve our handicap in the game of life. In this chapter, we'll study nine of the most important rules of coincidence.

1. There are things that like to happen together.
2. Thoughts are actions and produce effects.
3. Coincidence multiplies when we are in motion.
4. Life rhymes.
5. The world is a forest of symbols.
6. Every setback offers an opportunity.
7. To find our way, we may need to get lost.
8. Look for the hidden hand.
9. The passions of the soul work magic.

1. THERE ARE THINGS
THAT LIKE TO HAPPEN TOGETHER

Jung's theory of synchronicity may be flawed, but his life *practice* is a model of how to navigate with the help of coincidence and let the interweaving of inner and outer experience open a path to "absolute knowledge."

Jung had a little garden room on the lake, where he would often receive clients and colleagues in his later years. He would receive all the natural phenomena that were buzzing or splashing or sighing within his field of perception — the flight of insects, the wake of a boat, a shift in the wind — as a commentary on whatever was going on in his interaction with his visitor.

Jung's willingness to trust an unexpected incident — and accept it immediately as guidance for action — is evident in a meeting he had with Henry Fierz, who visited him in hopes of persuading him to support the publication of a manuscript by a recently deceased scientist. Jung had reservations about the book and opposed publication. The conversation became increasingly strained, and Jung looked at his watch, evidently getting ready to tell his guest he was out of time. Jung frowned when he saw the time.

"What time did you come?" he demanded of his visitor.

"At five o'clock, as agreed."

Jung's frown deepened. He explained that his watch had just been repaired, and should be keeping impeccable time. But it showed 5:05, and surely Fierz had been with him for much longer. "What time do you have?"

"Five thirty-five," his visitor told him.

"Since you have the right time and I have the wrong time," Jung allowed, "I must think again."

He then changed his mind and supported publication of the book.

We'll do well, in our daily practice, if we simply recognize that there are things that like to happen together, and allow those patterns to reveal themselves.

Look What's Going Down the Toilet

Shortly before the stock market crash in 1987, in the restroom on an airplane, I dropped a small wallet containing my credit card and checks from the brokerage account I had at that time — and only just managed to catch it before it vanished down the toilet.

Had this been a dream, I might have written a one-liner like: "If you're not very careful, your stock market investments will go down the toilet." Unfortunately, in 1987, I was not yet fully aware that incidents in waking life speak to us exactly like dream symbols. I failed to harvest the message, neglected to take the appropriate action to limit the risk to my brokerage account — and saw a large percentage of my net worth go down the toilet.

Three Geese in Flight

Nearly twenty years later — poorer but hopefully a little wiser — I was at the Iroquois Indian Museum in the rural Schoharie Valley of Upstate New York. I was giving an informal talk about my book *Dreamways of the Iroquois*, and I was gratified that the large audience included many people of the First Nations as well as many descendants of the first European settlers.

Afterward, a long line of people wanted me to sign their books.

A pleasant, mature woman sprang into action, finding seats for the older people and helping others to stay cheerful while they waited.

When things became less busy, she asked if she might sit and talk with me. Of course. She introduced herself with modest dignity. "I'm Freida Jacques. For twenty-seven years I have served as Mother of the Turtle Clan of the Onondaga people."

I felt honored and humbled to be in her presence.

She said, "I don't dream in the night so much, or don't remember. I dream like this. I need to know if I should accept an invitation to go out west, and I look up and there are three geese in flight, flying west like an arrowhead, with a hawk in front of them. Those three geese, the way they were flying, told me to go west."

A man waiting behind her couldn't restrain himself. He shoved his business card across the table. The name of his business was Three Geese in Flight, and he specialized in both Celtic and Iroquois books.

"That's very interesting," I told him. "Since I started dreaming in the Mohawk language, and studying Aboriginal peoples, some of my fierce Scottish ancestors have started walking through my dreams, basically saying, 'Look here, laddie. We know a thing also. Don't forget to talk to *us*.' Sometimes they say things in Scots Gaelic. I really don't know how I'm going to cope with that. Mohawk was bad enough."

Then a tall, lean, tweedy man waiting behind the bookseller couldn't hold back.

He pushed forward and gave me his hand.

"I'm a retired English professor," he told me. "I have devoted the rest of my life to preparing the definitive grammar of Scots Gaelic." He gave me his card. "If you need help translating those Gaelic words in your dreams, I'm your man, laddie."

2. THOUGHTS ARE ACTIONS
AND PRODUCE EFFECTS

It was Bonnie's final day as a curator at a historic site in New York. Retirement, after more than twenty years at a job she loved, was more than usually traumatic because it also meant moving out of the curator's cottage she had occupied for all that time. As she gathered her last things, a colleague asked Bonnie, "If you could take just one souvenir with you, after all these years, what would it be?"

Bonnie said at once, "Oh, I know the one thing I would want. But I can't have it."

"What is it?"

"An artist came here from New Hampshire, maybe fifteen years ago, and she painted my front garden when the colors were bright and perfect. I begged her for that painting — I offered to pay whatever she needed — but she wouldn't part with it. She said she never sold her favorite work."

As Bonnie told this story on her porch, a woman with a package made her way along the drive from the car park.

"You don't remember me," the woman said to Bonnie.

"Sorry."

"My name is Marilyn. I came here fifteen years ago and I painted your garden. You wanted the painting but I wouldn't sell it to you. But I woke up at four o'clock this morning knowing I had to drive here today and give it to you."

She handed Bonnie the package. When she tore off the paper, Bonnie found the painting she had just described.

Even with the evidence in her hands, it was hard for Bonnie to believe that the New England artist could have gotten up before dawn and driven across two states to hand her the picture — at the exact time she was about to leave the cottage forever. The logistics became a little easier to believe when the artist explained she no longer lived in New Hampshire; she had moved to within two hours' drive of the site Bonnie had helped to manage.

The incident is still amazing. How can it be explained?

I believe this is an example of how we reach to others, with our thoughts and feelings, even if we are oblivious to what we are doing. Mark Twain was a great student of phenomena of this kind.

He gathered his personal experiences and experiments in this area in a most interesting article he titled "Mental Telegraphy." He waited thirteen years to publish it, fearing ridicule or incredulity. When public interest and scientific research (notably the investigations of the young Society for Psychical Research in England) began to catch up with his own findings, he came out with the article in *Harper's Magazine*.

One of his favorite examples of the interplay of psyche and physics that generates coincidence is the phenomenon of "crossed letters." You know the kind of thing: you write to someone (or just think about them) — maybe someone you have not been in contact with for months — and then you get a letter or a call from that person the same day, or very soon after.

Twain noticed that again and again, when he wrote to someone, he would get a letter from that person that was mailed at or around the same time. He concluded that this was very often the effect of distant communication between minds keyed to similar wavelengths. His most extraordinary example is the Great Bonanza book.

One afternoon, Twain was seized with the passionate conviction that a great book could be written about the silver bonanza in Nevada. He felt his former newspaper colleague "Mr. Wright" would be the man to do it, but Twain was so possessed by the idea that he immediately roughed out an outline and sample chapters to get his old friend started. He was preparing to mail all this material to Wright when he received a package in the mail. Before opening the package, Twain told the people with him that he was going to deliver a "prophecy"; he declared that the package contained a letter from his old friend Wright, with *his* drafts for a book on the Great Bonanza. And so it did.

This incident convinced Twain not only that mental telegraphy is real but that it can be strong enough to transport the complete content of a book across three thousand miles. Fortunately,

Twain and Wright were good friends, and Twain had already determined that the Great Bonanza book was to be done by Wright; otherwise, the mental transfer (from Wright to Twain) could have resulted in two books and charges of plagiarism.

Minds resonate with each other, and in doing this, transfer ideas and messages back and forth. Twain was very interested to determine whether we could *pluck* the strings as well as wait for them to vibrate.

A case in point — from Twain's chronicle — involved an American on the grand tour in Europe who was desperate to receive news from his son, who was back in San Francisco and had not responded to his letters in many months. Twain urged the man to send a cable, which might sound like merest common sense. Here's the *un*common sense: Twain further told the worried father that it did not matter where he sent the cable. "Send it to Peking, if you like." All that mattered was that he should send a cable, and thereby send out a signal to the universe. If he did that, Twain promised, he would have news from his son right away.

The father sent the cable and the next day received a letter from his son explaining that he had left San Francisco months before on a slow boat and was now acting on his first opportunity to post a letter. The cable did not prompt the letter, which was mailed long before, but the two communications *coincided*, just as Twain had promised.

Twain developed what he was pleased to call a "superstition" about this. He decided that if he wanted to hear from someone, he would write that person a letter and then tear that letter up. Infallibly, he claimed, he would then receive a letter from the person to whom he had written. If this was "superstition," it was fresh-minted superstition and of a most practical kind; it worked.

Here is another story on the power of mental telegraphy, and since it involves me, I'll revert to the first person.

I was changing planes, yet again, wearing a suit because I had started leading seminars for businesspeople.

I took a seat at one side of a vast departure lobby. After a few moments, a woman jumped up from her seat on the far side and *ran* to me, heels clattering on the polished floor.

"Robert?"

"Yes"

"Robert *Moss*?"

"Uh-huh."

"I thought it was you, but I wasn't sure because I've never seen you in a suit. I went to a workshop with you twelve years ago and that experience changed my life. I was driving to the airport at Albuquerque this morning, and I said to my sister, 'As I approach retirement and try to figure out what the next stage of my life can be, there is one person I would most want to talk to — and that person is Robert Moss.'"

The woman's name was Suzanne, and we swapped seats on the plane so we could sit together. I was able to give Suzanne some insights on how to grow a vision for the next stage of her life and manifest the resources and opportunities to live that vision. In this way, Suzanne got exactly what she asked for, but in a way that cannot be explained by any obvious process of causation — though it may have been caused by factors working behind the scenes.

Mind Moves Matter

Minds not only reach to other minds; they move matter. The phrase "the mind moves matter" was coined over two thousand years ago by Virgil in the *Aeneid*. The engineers of the Eindhoven University of Technology in the Netherlands adopted the phrase, in the original Latin (*mens agitat molem*) as the motto of their institution. Engineers are practical people; they know this *works*.

Coincidence can be the result of psychokinesis, another name for mind moving matter. This may be intended or unintended. I'm fairly sure that Wolfgang Pauli did not, for the most part, intend to blow up laboratory equipment or cause other disturbances that came to be known as the Pauli Effect. But he came to enjoy his notoriety so much that one might suspect that he played the trickster at least half-consciously in his later years. In fact, he was given the role of Mephistopheles in a parody skit at a gala to celebrate the first ten years of Niels Bohr's physics institute in Copenhagen.

One more Pauli story: on the opening day of another prestigious institute — the C. G. Jung Institute in Zurich — the dignitaries were stunned when a huge Chinese vase flew off a table, for no apparent reason, at the precise moment that Pauli entered the room. The vase burst into fragments, causing a flood of water that put people to flight. Long afterward, Pauli played with the symbolic resonance of this event, noting several possible connections: the "Chinese" researches into the I Ching he had shared with Jung, the dreamlike association between a flood of water and an emotional outpouring, and the homophony between "flood" and "Fludd," the name of an alchemist Pauli had been studying.

3. COINCIDENCE MULTIPLIES WHEN WE ARE IN MOTION

Riffs of benign coincidence tend to come fastest at times of change, moments that stir the soul, when our passions are aroused — when we fall in love, or make a leap of faith, or are embarking on a new creative endeavor, or are close to birth or death. Coincidence multiplies when we are in motion, whether that is physical movement or the movement of our hearts and souls.

Serial coincidence may provide powerful confirmation of a path we are testing — or open a path about which we were previously unaware. Strings of coincidence can strengthen us in the determination to follow our deepest intuitions even when they run counter to conventional wisdom and logic and cannot be subjected to rational explanation. Like the exchange of secret handshakes between members of a fraternity, these signals alert us to the fact that we are not alone, that we have invisible sources of support, and that we are on the right course even when the whole world seems to be going the other way.

Love and danger are great triggers for coincidence. "The marvel is that I fled from Woman to *this* woman," sang Louis Aragon. "A vertiginous journey." Now, a forward movement of passion that strong is bound to exert a force field that will shift things in the environment!

"The greater the danger, the greater the saving power," wrote another poet, Hölderlin. Risk and danger also trigger unlikely sequences of events that sometimes leave us in no doubt that an invisible force has intervened in our lives.

On the other hand, negative synchronicities and countercurrents tend to multiply when we are resisting change or insisting on following an ego-driven agenda.

The easiest way to test this yourself is to make a date with coincidence when you are in transit, as I do when I fly on airplanes. Pay attention to what happens on the train, on the bus, in your car, or simply walking through the market, which has long been a fertile ground for meaningful chance.

The Marketplace Oracle

The Greeks thought a marketplace was a good place to go in order to pick up messages from the world. A popular oracle in ancient Greece, at Pharai in the Peloponnese, was located in a walled market. At the center of the market was a simple rough-hewn statue of Hermes, who plays messenger between gods and humans.

Consulting the oracle was as simple as this. You enter the market through the gate in the wall toward the close of business, as the vendors are packing up their stalls. You bring your question for the oracle with you. You walk to the statue of the god and whisper that question in his ear. Then you plug your ears, or press your hands over them, shutting out external sounds as you walk back to the gate. At the exact moment you reach the gate, you unplug your ears. The first sounds you hear — a snatch of conversation, the cry of a bird, the creak of an overloaded wagon — will be the response of the oracle. The god will speak to you directly through the everyday noise of the world, once you have set a clear intention and put yourself in a frame of mind to receive the message.

We can reinvent the oracle of Pharai in our own neighborhoods. Give yourself five minutes in your favorite supermarket — or one you have never visited before — with a question in mind and see what the world says to you. There are certain special markets where I particularly like to play this game, like the Santa Fe Flea Market and the Pike Place Market in Seattle. Ah, the market....

The Peach Factor

I am in Seattle; I wake up early and decide to take a morning stroll around the Pike Place Market. I notice that the produce stalls are bursting with fresh fruit; the peaches look especially ripe and juicy. I consider buying some fruit, but do not want to carry it back to the hotel. However, as I leave the market, I have second thoughts. I just have to sample some of those peaches. I choose Sosio's stall, where a sign above the mounds of fruit reads O MY GOD PEACHES. I joke with the vendor that the sign should actually read O MY GODDESS.

I now exit the market a couple of minutes later than I would have had I not gone back for the peaches.

As I walk along the street, a VW bug slows to match my pace. A woman's arm reaches out the driver's window and plucks at my sleeve. "O my God! Robert!" she cries. "You got me pregnant five months ago! We have to talk!"

I am so stunned I don't immediately recognize the woman in the car. She reminds me, as we move slowly along the street together, that she came to a workshop I led in Seattle five months before. At the time, she and her husband were trying to have a baby through in vitro fertilization. She reminds me that I helped her to journey to meet the soul of the incoming child, and to develop a ritual to add spiritual depth to the medical procedures. She tells me she feels that our work helped. Though she is forty-five and her doctors had anticipated difficulties, there have been none; she and her baby are happily on their way.

She is on her way to the market and asks if she can take me for coffee or breakfast to celebrate. She has a sudden craving for clams, and it requires some negotiation to get them at a restaurant at this early hour. As I watch her sucking down her clams, she tells me, "It's incredible meeting you here. I came for the peaches. Sosio's in the market is the best place in the world for peaches."

"I know," I smile, displaying my bag from Sosio's stand. "You came for the peaches and I came back for them."

She then tells me that she is going to buy two dozen O My God Peaches to make peach pies for a very special picnic — a picnic in a cemetery. She and several of her friends had lost close family in a tragic Alaskan Airlines crash a few years before. The survivors had agreed to hold a picnic, as well as a memorial service, to celebrate the dead and the living. As we speak, I feel the presence of her parents. Her father wants her to bury a personal item at his gravesite; I receive the clear impression of a corkscrew with a twisty wooden handle. I might feel awkward about passing on the message if synchronicity had not opened our path. She identifies the corkscrew immediately; it is a fine one with a vine root handle, one of many her father had collected. Since most of his body had vanished underwater, it feels right to lay something more of him in the earth on the occasion of the peachy picnic.

Everything that happened around the market that morning was charged with meaning. From the moment I bought the O My God Peaches, I seemed to have stepped out of ordinary time, into a deeper, juicier reality. The mother-to-be and I met because of the peaches, yet I took my walk with no thought of buying any kind of fruit, and the odds on our meeting in that way, with that connection, are beyond astronomical. There were important reasons for us to meet, involving birth and death.

But I was unaware of these at the time of our meeting, and had not thought of the mother-to-be since the workshop five months before, while on her side — though she had apparently had fond thoughts of me — she had no inkling that I was visiting her city that morning. Whatever brought us together was operating from far beyond the conscious mind, or any plausible notion of probability. As we enjoyed the shared sense that we had entered the play of larger forces, it seemed entirely natural that her parents should join the party — from the other side of death — to announce their wishes for the peachy picnic before it took place.

What is to be said about an episode like this? The first words that come to me are "*Thank you.*" The mother-to-be and I both felt blessed to have entered a realm of natural magic, where things operate according to dream logic, and the veil between the worlds thins.

Making a Double Magnet

Traveling in tandem with someone with whom you share a strong passion or a common interest can help to multiply your experience of coincidence, as if the two of you are becoming a double magnet, sending out a stronger traction beam than either of you might do individually.

In his remarkable memoir *L'Amour fou* ("Mad Love"), the surrealist poet and provocateur André Breton described an example of this doubling, from an experience of wandering around a Paris flea market with his friend the sculptor Alberto Giacometti. The sculptor was thinking about the undefined face of a woman in his current piece, and he found an odd mask that spoke to his need. Breton had developed an odd caprice; he wanted to have an ashtray made for him in the shape of a woman's high-heeled shoe. He found and purchased a curious wooden spoon in the flea market that had the identical shape, its handle resting on a woman's high heel.

Breton commented, "I would be tempted to say that two people walking near each other constitute a single influencing body, *primed*." He compares this phenomenon to "those sudden atmospheric condensations which make conductors out of regions that were not there before, producing flashes of lightning."

It *can* work like this, but let's be wary. Going around with someone else — or, certainly, in a group — can help to shut down your sensitivity to the signs and symbols around you, and may repel some of them. Why? Because we so often have the tendency to reinforce each other's long-standing attitudes and views of reality. For your friendship to be a coincidence multiplier, you both need to be in motion, and not just in the physical sense.

4. LIFE RHYMES

Mark Twain said that history may not repeat itself, but it rhymes. This is certainly true of personal history. Sometimes it's the little stories that make us aware that life rhymes. Consider this rhyming episode:

Cindy had a new boyfriend. After a year of not dating, followed by a succession of bad dates, she was thrilled to have found a man who filled her and fulfilled her. The sex was terrific, and she was thinking about it when she got on an office elevator, smiling to herself over the silly phrase she had uttered as she had kissed him good-bye: "You really are a hot dog."

Three men joined her in the elevator dressed in full-body hot-dog suits for a promotion. As the elevator went up, one of the giant wieners winked at Cindy and said, "If you're hungry, I'm available."

Here's another rhyming sequence in an ordinary day: I had an hour before my live radio show, whose theme that day was "What the Bleep Do We Know That We Don't *Know* We Know?"

I took the dog for a walk in a nearby park, thinking it would be cool if I noticed something that would give me a fresh anecdote on that theme. Just then, I noticed a flattened pack of Camel cigarettes on the path. Not exactly an exotic or uplifting sight, but it made me think of Egypt and camels.

After I returned to the house, my wife phoned to tell me her boss had just returned from a vacation in Egypt and had brought her a fabulous camel-bone bracelet. Then, when I got on the air, a caller told me she had been dreaming, night after night, about Egypt, and proceeded to describe one of her Egyptian dreams.

And another: As I was driving with family and friends to an evening concert, we heard the start of a Christmas-season message from a Catholic bishop who had been accused of soliciting young men in a local park.

"The bishop may not be an abuser, but he's a cruiser," someone quipped. "Turn him off."

I pushed the button for another station, and the first words we heard were "He has skeletons in his closet."

When there is rhyme, there are sometimes very interesting reasons. To experience these things fully, Baudelaire reminds us, we need to be in a state of "poetic health."

Black Dog on the Plane

I flew to the West Coast with my friend Wanda Burch, who had just published her book *She Who Dreams*, about her path to healing from breast cancer through Active Dreaming. I spoke to Wanda on the plane about the important role that black dogs have played in my life and in my dreams and how the black dog often figures in mythology as a gatekeeper or guide.

As we disembarked at Chicago's O'Hare Airport, Wanda said, "There was a black dog on the plane." I turned and saw a large black standard poodle and its owner, a striking fair-haired woman, disembarking. I would have stopped to talk to them, but Wanda and I had to hurry to make our connection.

As we were standing in line at the departure gate, Wanda said, "There's the black dog again." I started to walk over to introduce myself when I heard my name being paged. When I got to the check-in desk, the airline clerk asked me, "Would you mind sitting next to a dog on the plane?" I told her I would be delighted.

On board the plane, I swapped seats with the poodle's owner to give the dog room to stretch out. I now found myself sitting between Wanda and the dog's owner, who turned out to be a surgeon who specialized in breast cancer patients. The surgeon told me she was originally from Wanda's part of the country — the Mohawk Valley — but had moved to Palo Alto.

When I introduced the two women, the surgeon was greatly interested in Wanda's use of dreams for self-diagnosis and healing, and she wanted to know whether her doctors had been willing to listen to her dreams. Wanda praised one of her oncologists, whom she called "Doctor Bart" in her book, for his active interest in her dreams.

"*Doctor Bart?*" the surgeon echoed, incredulous. "He called me last week. He invited me to return to the Mohawk Valley to take over his practice."

The Shark Shows His Fin

The next story unfolded the very next day. The setting was Seattle. The black dog theme came up again. So did a shark's fin.

I was driving with friends to the Fox TV station in downtown Seattle for a live interview. We had a few minutes to spare, so we crossed the highway on foot to get a cup of coffee. There was so much traffic as we tried to recross the busy road that we began to worry we would be late for the show. Then the driver of a strange car braked in the middle of the highway and waved for me to cross. The car was amazing. It was painted in roaring waves of blue and green, and on top was a giant shark fin.

I wondered if this was setting a theme for the breakfast show. One thing I know about sharks is that they don't get cancer. I have worked with cancer patients to transfer the healing image of a shark that can gobble up cancer cells like an aquatic Pac-Man, and sometimes this has done great good.

As I waited in the studio, the story rolling across the TV screens was about a black dog that — through a bizarre chain of circumstance — had inherited millions of dollars. I noted a rhyming theme from the plane flight the day before.

My interview began, and the anchorwoman told me a personal dream, in which she was flying over Caribbean waters. Looking down, she saw the dorsal fins of sharks circling in the water below her.

I asked for her feelings, and she said she felt happy inside the dream. I suggested that, if this were my dream, I might see it as holding a promise of healing from cancer for someone I knew, because sharks don't get cancer. The anchorwoman gasped and said she had just received news that her mother was on the mend from cancer. She added that she had the dream when she was on vacation in the Caribbean, which was also when her mother was first diagnosed with cancer. There was total silence in the newsroom after this exchange.

After the show, we took the ferry across to Vashon Island to check out a possible site for future workshops. The owner was agitated because of a shark dream she had had the night before — and because that same morning, she had discovered that some special shark teeth she kept next to her bed had gone missing.

5. THE WORLD IS A FOREST OF SYMBOLS

The phrase comes from Baudelaire:

Nature's a temple where living columns
Sometimes deliver messages in riddles;
Man makes his way through forests of symbols
That watch him with intimate knowledge.

Everything that enters our field of perception means *something*, large or small. Everything speaks to us, if we will take off our headphones and hear a different sound track. Everything corresponds.

We travel better in the forest of symbols when we are open and *available* to all the forms of meaning that are watching and waiting for us. We travel best when we can manage that sense of rhythm and rhyme that Baudelaire called "a poetic state of health." The celebrated ancient Greek authority on dreams, Artemidorus of Daldis, said that the great requirement for a successful dream interpreter is "a gift for resemblances." This is the

key for reading the symbols that are watching us along the trails
of ordinary life, and the gift grows with practice.

The signs that come up are sometimes unmistakably in our
face. Kathy was fuming over the angry breakup of a relationship
when she noticed that the woman driver ahead of her who was
running a red light had the following bumper sticker: "I use ex-
lovers for speed bumps." Kathy had to laugh. That so exactly reflected her mood, while also inviting her to take a look at herself
and lighten up.

But the very nature of a symbol is to carry us beyond what
we know to what we do not yet know (or remember), and for this
reason the meaning and valence of symbols is often obscure to the
little, everyday mind. So how do we learn to read those "messages
in riddles" (*confuses paroles*)? Through practice. There are two
forms of practice, in this connection, that I recommend highly.
The first is to look at the incidents of daily life as if they were
dream symbols. The second is to develop a personal set of markers you can use as road signs after you have tested them.

Look at the Incidents of Daily Life as Dream Symbols

We need to take dreams more literally and the incidents of waking life more symbolically.

If we dream of a house or a car, a dream analyst will often encourage us to think about what is going on with the house or the
car as an analog for something that is unfolding — or stuck — in
our psyches or our bodies. If there's a problem with the furnace,
you might then want to ask how your heart is troubled.

I've found this approach helpful in working with dreams —
though the dream house may also refer to our literal house, or be
a home in another reality altogether. However, I find it even more
interesting to consider the condition of our literal house or car in
a symbolic way.

For instance, a man who was driving himself very hard at the office had three flat tires in a single week. The third time, he heard the pun. A problem with a "tire" might have to do with getting over-"tired." When he realized that, he also noticed he had been getting increasingly short of breath. He decided to pace himself and ease off in "tiring" situations.

As we were approaching the closing in the sale of a house where I had lived and written for a decade, I looked for a tie to wear to the lawyer's office. However, I couldn't find any ties in my wardrobe in the new house. I then realized that — although we had moved everything out of the old place and checked and rechecked that it was empty and broom-clean — I must have left my tie rack on the door in the master bedroom.

We made a detour on the drive to the lawyer's office so I could get my old ties out of the old place. It was not too hard to see the dreamlike symbolism here. Selling a house (or getting a divorce, or quitting your job) does not automatically break the old ties. You want to make sure you are not leaving yourself psychically and emotionally "tied" to an old situation, even as you move physically beyond it.

Practice Your Secret Handshakes with the World

As we travel through our forest of symbols, we'll start to notice recurring signs that point to something that lies on the road ahead, out of ordinary sight. These signs may be telling us it's going to be a great day, that we're on the right track, or that something fabulous is about to manifest. Or they may warn of danger, when the best thing we can do is get back in bed and put our heads under the covers.

These signs, of course, are secret handshakes from the world. We want to practice squeezing back, with just the right movements and pressure. This means getting to recognize your own personal markers and testing them.

There is a forest people in northern Zaire for whom travel is very perilous. There are predators in the jungle — the humans worse than the animals — as well as landslides, floods, and broken rope bridges. These people are always on the lookout for markers to tell them whether it's wise or safe to travel on a given day. They pay attention, among other things, to involuntary signs from their own bodies. You stub your toe, and that is good or bad depending on whether the toe is on your left foot or your right foot. You sneeze, and again that is a good sign or a bad sign depending on whether most of the air is coming out of your lucky nostril or your unlucky nostril. Which is which? In the teachings of this forest people, nobody can tell you that. You find out by trial and error. You stub your left big toe, say, and you see how the trip works out. If you get to the next village safely, and your business is profitably concluded, and nobody robs you on the way home, you may conclude that your left toe is your lucky toe. But you'll need to test this again to make sure. You have to be willing to stub your toe a few times — and then check the outcome during the rest of the day or the whole of the trip — to get this right.

Superstition? Maybe. But if this is superstition, it's of a personal and practical kind.

I'm not sure which is my lucky toe, but I know about lucky birds and animals — meaning those that are lucky for me.

I have no problem with black birds in general, but if I see a solitary crow or raven flying away to my left, I take that as a sign to watch out for something going wrong that day.

Back in the mid-1980s, tired of big cities and the commercial fast track I'd been on, I was considering a move to a rural location in the upper Hudson Valley of New York. Through an interesting riff of coincidence, my wife and I were shown a large piece of land with a falling-down farmhouse that *might* be coming on the market in the near future. I sat with a great white oak behind the house, thinking about this possible opportunity. Fixing the house might open a "money pit," and there were a bunch of other calculations, and yet this place seemed deeply right. I had always loved oak trees, and sitting with this great white oak, I felt deeply at home. Yet I wanted another sign, an unmistakable handshake from the world.

A red-tailed hawk came circling overhead, speaking to me urgently in a language I knew I would be able to understand — if only I spoke hawk. She swooped lower, sunlight glinting on her silver-white belly plumage. And she dropped a wing feather between my legs.

Did I buy the farm? You bet.

Since then, I track the movements of red-tailed hawks whenever they appear in a landscape. If the hawk is flying my way, or hunting successfully, I know I am on the right track.

Every Moment Is a Learning Opportunity

When we understand that the world is a book of symbols, we may come to grasp that every moment is a learning opportunity, in absolutely any situation.

While I was exploring this theme, a book came tumbling out of a teetering pile — one of many — in my house. I picked it up, alert to a possible intervention by the Library Angel, and found it was a "mirror for princes," a book of guidance that a medieval philosopher-prince on the border of Persia composed for his son.

I found amazing insights here, including a thought that speaks directly to our theme of seizing every opportunity to read the symbols of the world. Kai Ka'us advised his son: "Do not appoint any particular time for learning; whatever the time or the circumstances, not a moment should be allowed to lapse without your learning something."

6. EVERY SETBACK OFFERS AN OPPORTUNITY

The genesis of the wildly successful ABC television series *Desperate Housewives* is a marvelous example of how when we find one door blocked, another may be ready to open. Scriptwriter Marc Cherry was out of work, at his mother's place watching a TV news report on Andrea Yates, the young mother convicted of drowning her children in a bathtub. He turned to his mother, horrified, and asked, "Can you imagine being so desperate you would do that to your children?" His mother removed the cigarette from her mouth and said, "I've been there." Cherry had his title, before he had written a word of the script.

He developed a script and gave it to his agent. She showed it to several networks, and they all turned it down. Then his agent was charged with embezzling from her clients, including Cherry. He found a new agent, who saw his project as "a soap opera with dark comedy potential," and it sold it right away.

Getting to Know the Gatekeeper

If we can manage not to spend too much time feeling sorry for ourselves, or raging over what has gone wrong, we have a chance of finding opportunity in almost any setback. Of course this can be hard to grasp when we have lost something very dear to us, or are staring bankruptcy in the face, or are suffering a terrible illness.

In the darkest moments of my life, I sometimes try on one or both of these statements: *What does not kill me makes me stronger* and *The fire that melts the butter tempers the steel.*

Both phrases are from Nietzsche. When I can say one or both of those lines without rebelling or recoiling inside my body, I know I'm ready to go looking for the opportunity that is waiting for me — ready to turn my attention from any past history of failure and disappointment toward a new horizon.

When I do that, I sometimes notice that what has been blocking me or pushing me back feels like a personal force — and is personal in a sense that goes beyond any other personalities involved in the situation.

I think of this force as the Gatekeeper. He (he is male for me; maybe female for you) is actively engaged in opening and closing doors and roads in life. He is honored by various names in various cultures, but we don't need those names here.

All we need to appreciate is that by entering into a conscious connection with our personal Gatekeeper, we might find it easier to find the right openings, especially when the road has seemed to be closed.

At a certain passage in my life, I was exhausting myself trying to push through a certain project that seemed to be terminally blocked. I felt I was beating on a solid door that simply would not open.

Flopped down in an easy chair, trying for a short nap, I suddenly saw my situation with dreamlike objectivity. There I was, trying to beat down that door. The door was studded with metal, and my knuckles were turning bloody as I kept on trying to break it down.

Then I felt a shiver — truth comes with goosebumps — and looked in a different direction. I saw that there was an open archway quite near to me. Beyond it were beautiful gardens and (it seemed to me) all manner of earthly delights. Standing in the archway was an elegant but tricksterish figure who seemed familiar, beckoning to me. I moved toward his crooked finger and through the archway into the garden of delights. I had lost my witness perspective, ready to enjoy myself.

Yet I needed to see the larger picture. I looked back, trying to understand what was going on here, and I noticed two things. While the Gatekeeper in my fantasy had been beckoning me with one hand, he had been using the other to hold that studded door closed against me. And what was behind that door I had thought it so important to go through was a space like a jail cell, a place of confinement.

As a result of this vision, I abandoned a commercial project I had been trying to develop and decided to give my full energies to riskier creative work that did not offer an obvious way to pay the bills — but it eventually did that, and far more.

I've come to believe that some of the blocks and setbacks we encounter in life are placed on our paths by our Gatekeeper to save us from compounding mistakes, to make us take a longer view of our issues — and encourage us to shift direction and notice better options.

7. TO FIND OUR WAY, WE MAY NEED TO GET LOST

Appian of Alexandria was a famous historian in the heyday of the Roman Empire. He wrote in Greek, but was a Roman citizen and very definitely one of the ruling caste.

So when a violent rebellion broke out in Roman-ruled Egypt in the time of Trajan, Appian was one of those targeted by the rebels — Jews who believed that a new messiah had come. He fled across the marshes of the Nile Delta, with an Arab guide, heading for a ship that was waiting for him on one of the branches of the river. He had arranged for the ship to take him to safety in the port of Pelusium.

Appian and his guide traveled all night through the marshes. At dawn, a crow shrieked and the guide said, "We are lost."

The crow squalled again, and the Arab said grimly, "We are utterly and completely lost."

Appian, believing his life was at risk and that his pursuers were close behind, fell into despair.

The crow shrieked for a third time. The Arab's expression

turned to complete joy. "Ah, but it is such good luck that we became lost. There is a shortcut just ahead."

Though Appian may not have understood this, he was fortunate to have a guide who knew the language of crows. In many traditions, crows are messengers, and close attention is paid to their actions.

The Arab led the way decisively, and very soon they came to a branch of the Nile and saw a galley in full sail. However, this was not the expected meeting place nor the same ship on which Appian had arranged passage.

"Where are you going?" Appian called to the captain.

"Pelusium!" the captain called back.

Of course, Appian boarded the galley, which carried him to Pelusium safely. By his own account, his life was saved because he got lost and took the "wrong" boat. The ship that had been engaged to take him to Pelusium was captured by the rebels, and its passengers and crew were held as prisoners or killed.

Sometimes we must get lost in order to find the right way.

The Navigational Law of Serendipity

This is the cardinal navigational law of serendipity: You can only get to the magic kingdom by getting lost. You get there when you think you are going somewhere else and fall off the maps.

The eighteenth-century writer Horace Walpole imported the word *serendipity* into the English language after reading a Persian story in which traveling princes were "always making discoveries, by accidents and sagacity, of things which they were not in quest of." In Walpole's lexicon, serendipity is thus the effect of "accidental sagacity."

In the story of his sixth voyage, Sindbad the Sailor gets hopelessly lost, is overwhelmed by a terrible storm, and is shipwrecked on an alien shore — to discover that he has been washed up on the wonderful island of Serendib, a place of incredible beauty and riches. Our word *serendipity* is derived from the name of that magical island. As in the story, we find this land only by getting lost.

Such episodes abound in the literal history of world exploration. Leif Eriksson, who may have been the first European to set foot in North America, got there while trying to outrun a storm. Christopher Columbus famously discovered a new continent while looking for a new way to somewhere else — India.

"Accidental Sagacity" in Science and Invention

Serendipity is a major factor in scientific discovery and invention, as in exploration, successful military command, and entrepreneurship. Alfred Nobel produced gelignite — a more stable explosive than dynamite, which he also invented — when he accidentally mixed collodium (gun cotton) with nitroglycerin. Swiss chemist Albert Hoffmann discovered the properties of LSD by accidentally ingesting it at his lab.

Here is a quick inventory of some other important or well-known inventions and products that were the gift of "accidental sagacity":

Alexander Fleming discovered penicillin because he neglected to isolate bacterial cultures from stray spores blowing around in his hospital building — notably from a mycologist's lab on the floor below. Fleming went away on vacation. When he returned, he found that penicillin mold had killed his bacteria — and saw with his trained eye an extraordinary cure.

Rayon was discovered by the French chemist Hilaire de Chardonnet, an assistant to Louis Pasteur, when he spilled a bottle of collodion and later noticed that as the liquid evaporated, it changed into a viscous substance from which thin fibers could be drawn.

Charles Goodyear learned how to vulcanize rubber — producing the automobile tire and spawning the automotive revolution in transportation — after he accidentally left a mixture on a hot plate that turned into hard rubber.

The secret of America's favorite breakfast cereal was discovered when the Kellogg brothers left cooked wheat untended for a day, and then found that when they tried to roll the mass, they got flakes instead of a sheet.

The glue that makes Post-it notes possible was accidentally discovered by a scientist who was trying to produce a strong adhesive, but developed a very weak one instead.

The secret of ink-jet printers was discovered by a Canon engineer when he accidentally placed a hot soldering iron on his pen — and then saw ink jetting from the pen's tip a few moments later.

Finally, Viagra was originally tested as a drug to help with hypertension and angina. Clinical trials revealed that it did not do much for angina, but it had a marked effect on another physical condition in males.

Notice that more than "dumb luck" was involved in these inventions and discoveries. The people responsible for them were able to add "sagacity" — skill, experience, and practical imagination — to "accidents," thus becoming true exemplars of what Walpole called "accidental sagacity." To put it another way, they were prepared to get lucky. As Louis Pasteur remarked, "Chance favors the prepared mind."

The accidents and missteps that provided the vital clues would have been ignored — except as triggers for curses and complaints — by anyone except the prepared, creative, questing minds that saw the magic in apparent mistakes.

It may be that inventors and creators *attract* the right kind of accidents. In *Fire in the Crucible*, his study of creative genius, John

Briggs rightly observed that "Creators actively court chance. They're always ready to notice and amplify with insight some accident of their environment virtually everybody else thinks is trivial or fails to notice. This capacity is, in a deep sense, what makes creators creative."

8. LOOK FOR THE HIDDEN HAND

I was walking with a friend in the New Forest in Hampshire. We were both undergoing major life changes, which is not always smooth sailing. We had had a major row the night before, drinking too much and bumping up against darker sides of each other's personalities. Now we were walking, detoxifying, working it through. We walked all day, traveling fifteen or twenty miles on those forest trails, losing track of distance and — we finally noticed — direction. England may be a rather small country, but the New Forest is not a small wood. We looked at each other and laughed, realizing that in our effort to find ourselves, we had become utterly lost.

I said out loud, "I wish a guide would just appear out of nowhere and show us the way. Wouldn't that be fabulous?"

My friend laughed like a crow. We had seen no one in the forest that day.

But within a minute or two, a runner appeared on our trail. He waved to us cheerily. "You two look lost. Need some help?"

"Yes, please."

"Mustn't break my stride. I'll leave you markers."

A minute later, he had vanished in the dappled wood. We followed his lead. At the next fork in the trail, we found he had indeed left a marker — an arrow formed with three sticks — showing us the right way to go. We found a succession of these arrows at every crossing or forking of the trail, along the whole two-mile distance back to the main road.

The Gods Love to Travel in Disguise

The Greeks say the gods love to travel in disguise. In Greek folk tradition, it's good policy to be nice to strangers, and to pay attention to what they say, because you never know who is traveling behind their masks.

On another visit to England, I landed at Heathrow on a red-eye flight, exhausted and burdened with financial worries. I was carrying too much baggage and had to wrestle an oversize suitcase down the steps to the Underground.

As I collapsed onto a seat on the train, a roly-poly man, bearded like Santa Claus, *winked* at me from the seat opposite. He said with a broad grin, "The Buddha says — walk on the bridge, don't build on it."

The words slapped me in the face. They stung me awake. They were exactly what I needed to hear. Caught up in my immediate worries, stressed out and overtired, I had been forgetting one of the secrets of living the Incredible Journey: it's the journey, not the destination, that counts.

The stranger on the London Tube was an example of how we play everyday angels — even gods in disguise — for each other. There is a provocative Buddhist text on this theme entitled *Entry into the Realm of Reality* (in the Thomas Cleary translation). It describes how authentic spiritual teachers — even the greatest who walk this earth — can appear in any guise, as an exotic dancer or as a monk, as a panhandler or a king, as a scholar or a warrior.

We are most likely to run into them when we are in motion, especially when we are crossing a border into unfamiliar territory, when strong emotions are in play, and when we are facing the greatest challenges. They take many forms.

For me, a friendly black dog — especially when it appears in an unlikely place — is a good omen, and sometimes I detect a hint of a superior being traveling in disguise.

As I arrived once at the Fort Mason conference center in San Francisco, on the first morning of a weekend workshop, I wondered if the world would give me a sign of how the program was likely to go.

Our meeting space was a converted firehouse right on the water. As I walked from the parking lot toward the building, a large man in a bright red watchcap appeared right in front of the doors. He was walking a standard black poodle — unclipped, of course.

When we greeted each other, I told him why I was glad to see him with his big black dog, at the gate of our adventure.

He told me the name of his black dog was "Pollo. Short for Apollo."

Albert's Hash

The gods are not the only ones who travel in disguise. Sometimes — as in the story in the introduction of the woman auditor who believed her mother helped her to get her truck — we feel the hand of a departed loved one in the workings of coincidence.

A friend told me she had been dreaming about her father's death while her father was still very much alive. More precisely, she had been dreaming *beyond* his death, previewing family conversations that might take place some days or weeks after the event. The dreams had a just-so quality. Since we were both well aware of how dreams often rehearse families for a death, we agreed to discuss how she might use these dreams to help prepare her father and others in the family for his *big* journey, and so we met over breakfast at a popular local diner, the Pancake Corral.

On the way to the diner, I asked whether there was anyone in the father's family who had already passed over that he might regard as a friend and guide. "Oh yes," my friend responded at once. "There's Uncle Albert." She explained that her father had loved his elder brother Albert, who had died three years earlier, and he had been shocked when Albert had showed up — "like a friendly ghost" — in his bedroom a week after his death.

We were talking about Uncle Albert as we entered the diner. The place was crowded, and my friend gave my name to the hostess to put on the wait list. "Albert!" the hostess said loudly, writing down the dead uncle's name instead of mine.

"I think Albert just gave us a nudge," I joked.

Later that same day, during my workshop, my friend and I agreed to make a conscious dream journey in hopes of contacting Albert. She had quite a long interview with her uncle. I met him, but he was not especially interested in talking to me since I was not family. He did confide that what *he* liked for breakfast was corned beef hash, and that he also liked peach brandy.

When I relayed this information to my friend, she was unable to confirm whether these were, in fact, her uncle's preferences.

We got a message about that when we returned to the diner two days later. I told the server I didn't need to see the menu; I would have what I had the previous time. "You might want to take a look," she said. "They've added a new item for the first time since I've been working here."

I looked at the menu. The new item was corned beef hash. *Albert's breakfast.*

My friend decided to talk to her father. She did not tell him the whole sequence, and she did not say that she had dreamed of his death. She said only that she had been dreaming about Uncle Albert. She asked if Albert had liked corned beef hash. "Al *loved* hash!" her father exclaimed. "He asked for it every time he could." How about peach brandy? "He drank peach brandy every night before he went to sleep."

The Mingling of Minds

William Butler Yeats observed that when our minds are working on a challenging line of inquiry, we attract the interest of other and deeper intelligences. This may lead to a "mingling of minds" in which our inner and outer discoveries are supported by past masters in our chosen field.

This evokes my dream of the place of the dead presidents (told in the introduction), in which former statesmen were joining their energies and wisdom to present leaders.

Yeats discovered something very important about this kind of interaction: we feed and entertain spiritual helpers and mentors through our reading and chosen studies. Yeats accepted reading assignments from "spirit instructors."

> I read with an excitement I had not known since I was a boy with all knowledge before me, and made continual discoveries, and if my mind returned too soon to their unmixed abstraction they would say, "We are starved."

When we approach books with this fervor, that benign entity that Arthur Koestler called the Library Angel becomes more and more active, ensuring that the book we need appears, or falls open at the right page, just when we need it.

9. THE PASSIONS OF THE SOUL WORK MAGIC

The stronger the emotion, the stronger its effect on our psychic and physical environment. And the effects of our emotions may reach much further than we can initially understand. They can generate a convergence of incidents and energies, for good or bad, in ways that change *everything* in our lives and can affect the lives of many others.

We have already seen that when we think or feel strongly about another person, we *will* touch that person and affect their mind and body — even across great distances — unless that person has found a way to block that transmission. The great French novelist Honoré de Balzac, who knew a great deal about these things, wrote that "ideas are projected as a direct result of the force by which they are conceived and they strike wherever the brain sends them by a mathematical law comparable to that which directs the firing of shells from their mortars."

Scientific experiments have shown the ability of the human mind and emotions to change physical matter: studies by Masuru Emoto have shown that human emotions can change the nature and composition of water, and the Findhorn experiments have taught us that good thoughts positively affect the growth of plants. Conversely, rage or grief can produce disturbing and sometimes terrifying effects in the physical environment. Many of us know people who stop watches or blow up computers when their emotions are running high and uncontrolled. That's just the start of it. An angry person can be a fire starter. I've seen major fires generated by the force of someone's violent rage. I've seen punishing windstorms and freak, localized snowstorms generated in a similar way. These things don't just happen in Stephen King novels.

So let's talk about passion.

Our passions can lead us into madness. They can also give us the creative edge to do our best and most original work, and the magnetism that generates extraordinary opportunities and serendipity.

The passions of the soul work magic. This observation, attributed to the great Dominican scholar and magus Albertus Magnus (and loved by Jung), is possibly the most *practical* sentence you will read in this book.

There are two conditions for working positive magic this way.

The first is that we must *choose* to take the primal, pulsing energy of our strongest passions and direct it toward a creative goal. The passion that is throbbing and surging inside us may be love or lust (or both), the fierce desire to give birth or the desperate wish to end it all. The passion may be wild rage or terrible grief. Whatever its origin, the strongest passions of the soul produce the energy to remake our world — if we choose to direct that energy. Imagine a vast body of pent-up water, engorged by a pounding thunderstorm, that is going to burst through a dam with irresistible power. We can choose to harness that force, turning it into hydroelectric power that can light our city and warm our homes. Or we can let it swamp everyone and everything in its path, bringing misery and devastation.

The second requirement for letting the passions of the soul work magic is that we must seize the moment when they are running strongest and give ourselves completely to acting in the power of that moment. The time is always *now*, but when the passions of the soul are at work the time is also *go*. I know this as a writer. Often my best work is done when I am in a state of great turmoil, when my passions are running strong but my heart and mind are also conflicted. Such moments give us an edge. I know, from experience, that my best and most original work can come through *now* — if I use that edge and make myself available to the work *any* time it is coming through. In these states, like Balzac, I often write for fifteen hours a day, fueled only by coffee, and sleep only a couple of hours out of the twenty-four — and stream into joy, the joy we all know when we are in the zone, whatever our field of endeavor, and are giving our best.

Balzac was a master in his literary depiction of the workings of passion and desire. He understood the fundamental unity of mind and matter, and that there is a law of *spiritual* gravitation as well as a law of physical gravitation. His view of reality — and his prodigious literary production — were driven by a vitalist belief in the power of will and imagination. His early novel *Louis Lambert* is a tale of the strange life of a young explorer in consciousness who is awakened by a precognitive dream to the fact that the world is much deeper than can be explained by reason and Newtonian physics. He comes to believe that man can become a creator by *concentrating* a whole reality — even an entire world — inside himself, re-visioning it, and then *projecting* the new image to fill his environment. But the protagonist comes unstuck and unhinged because he can't ground his understanding in the physical world.

The Balzacian hero is a man of desire and imagination who must also ground his passions in the body, in healthy sex, in social engagement with the world — or else go mad.

Balzac's version of what becomes possible through exercising the passions of the soul is wonderful. Acts of mind, fueled by passion, abolish time and space. "To desire is immediately to be where one desires to be, instantaneously to be what one desires to be." Time is devoured by the moment; space is absorbed by the point. "For the man in such a state, distances and material objects do not exist, or are traversed by a life within us."

What kind of desire makes these things possible? "A desire is a fact entirely accomplished in our will before being accomplished externally." The passion that works magic is "the will gathered to one point" so that "man can bring to bear his whole vitality."

A person who carries a great desire is surrounded by a certain "atmosphere," a "magnetic fluid" that moves in waves, like sound and light, and touches others. That person produces "a contagion of feelings." Passion of this kind magnifies sensory abilities; we can see and hear and sense things vividly across distance.

Coincidences multiply around such a person because things now happen through "sympathies which do not recognize the laws of space."

ASKING the EVERYDAY ORACLE

It is deep December, and I am worried about a situation that seems to offer no happy outcome. I am walking around the lake in the local park, past a beautiful lakehouse festooned with Christmas snowmen. The sunlight glints on green water. As I follow the winding path, I notice that the city has put up signs on many of the trees that border the lake. The signs caution DO NOT CROSS. BEWARE OF THIN ICE.

The dissonance hits me after I have read this message half a dozen times.

Because we are having an unusually mild December, the lake has not yet frozen. In fact, there is no snow or ice to be seen anywhere in the park. The announcement is premature.

Then something more exciting hits me. *I have just been given a message by the world*. Actually, there are two of them. The one that gives me hope is: don't assume this situation is frozen. The one that gives me caution is on the literal sign: *Beware of thin ice*.

Thin ice can mean more than ice on a lake.

The Romans paid a great deal of attention to the way the world speaks to us through natural phenomena and odd little daily incidents and signs that are all around us, waiting to be noticed at the right moment. The Romans distinguished between two broad categories of omen: those that are given (*omina oblativa*) and those that are provoked (*omina impetrativa*). The message in the THIN ICE signs was something that popped up uninvited, a simple gift from the world.

When I sat down at the end of that walk in the park, I decided to cast the I Ching to "provoke" an omen. I threw a fearsome hexagram, number 29, the Abyss. The ideogram shows a human figure falling into a chasm. The pattern of water upon water evokes a tremendous life storm. The commentary says, "You'll only get through by following your truth and your heart."

But there are three changing lines in the hexagram, and they produce what readers of the Chinese oracle call the "secondary" hexagram. This is number 64, the final hexagram in the cycle, and its name is Not Yet Over. The picture that comes is of a crossing that has not yet been completed. We're at the end of a whole cycle, but everything is still in play. Every ending is a beginning. The counsel that comes with this hexagram includes the line: "Move like an old fox on thin ice."

In this episode, I was given a spontaneous message from the world, and then provoked one, a further example of how life rhymes.

PUTTING YOUR QUESTION TO THE WORLD

Here's another story about "provoking" an answer from the world.

Sheila told us in one of my beginners' classes that she had stopped remembering her dreams. When gently questioned, she admitted that this was probably because she feared her dreams were telling her something unpleasant she preferred not to think about — the possibility that she was going to lose her job.

I asked Sheila to write down the theme on which she needed guidance. Her theme, of course, was: "Am I going to lose my job?"

I invited her to play the Coincidence Game. I said, "Carry that question with you. Then pretend that the first unusual or unexpected thing that enters your field of perception is a personal message to you from the universe, containing the answer to your question."

I saw Sheila one week later in the next class.

She couldn't wait to tell us what had happened. "I got my answer as soon as I walked out of the building that night. I know the area very well, but somehow I found myself driving the wrong way down a one-way street for three or four blocks. I wouldn't have noticed even then except a truck driver put on his high beams and leaned on his air horn."

"So the message was...?"

"I've been driving the wrong way down a one-way street. My job is blown."

Clarity is good; a plan is even better. Sheila proceeded to report that no sooner had she gotten the message about her job than her dream drought broke. She dreamed she was at a conference on transportation in Washington, DC. There was a sense of promise in this dream, although the content mystified her since, as she told us, "I know nothing about transportation except how to drive the wrong way down a one-way street."

As we explored the dream, running a reality check on what Sheila recognized from it in her waking life, we discovered that (1) she had a close friend in Washington, DC, and (2) her main job skill was organizing conferences.

I asked her for an action plan. She said, "I have some frequent-flyer miles. I'll use them to fly to Washington, DC, stay with my friend, and scope out the prospects."

A month later, she quit her job and moved to a higher-paying job in Washington, DC — which was just as well, since six months later the department where she had worked was abolished. Her new job essentially involved arranging conferences, including the conference on transportation she had dreamed.

Five-Minute Oracle: Putting Your Question to the World

To play this game, you first need to come up with a clear intention. I find it easiest to get clarity if I frame my intention by filling in the blank in the following simple statement: "I would like guidance on..."

What you put in that blank should be something that really matters. Don't worry about whether or not your intention is spiritually important or earth-shattering. Make it snappy. Let it be authentic. Listen to your heart and your gut.

Quick — what do you *really* need help or guidance with?

If it's love or money, then say so. If it's what to wear on a date, or whether you should call someone to make a date, that's perfectly fine. On the other hand, don't be scared to express one of the *big* themes. If the first thing that comes is "I would like guidance on my life purpose," then go with that.

Once you've expressed your intention, the game is to pretend that the next striking or unusual thing that enters your field of perception is a direct message to you from the universe. That message may come right away, as it did for Sheila. Or you may need to do something active in order to inspire it.

Here are a few suggestions:

Take a ride or a walk. As we've observed, coincidence multiplies when we are in motion. Maybe your message is in the vanity plate on the car in front of you, or the fact that it's an Illinois plate with the slogan Land of Lincoln.

Play the car radio game. Pretend the first song or commercial that comes on is the guidance you are seeking.

Play the book-skimming game. Open a book at random. Pretend the first passage that leaps to your eye contains your message from the universe.

If the message you get is clear, you're done! You have your five-minute oracle.

If the message is ambiguous or a total mystery, well, that's how oracles stay in business. You may need help in relating the message you received to your original intention. Consider asking others to use their imaginations to help you with this, as in the Coincidence Card Game (see below).

Then again, you may not *want* to hear the message you receive. Many years ago, when I was developing *three* business projects, I played the car radio game. What came on right away was a commercial for *three* funeral homes. And I thought, this is not the message I want. Funeral homes are for things that are dead. The universe is telling me my three business ideas are dead before they've been born. I wriggled and twisted, trying to get away from that clear message. But by the end of the week, I had to accept that the car radio counsel was spot on: those three oh-so-clever projects were dead.

Five-Minute Oracle: Let the World Put the Question to You

Putting Your Question to the World can be a wonderfully revealing exercise, whether it's confirming or chastening. But it's sometimes more magical to enjoy coincidence *au naturel*. We may not actually know what question to ask, and the world — like our dreams — may have more to tell us than is on our minds.

Here's how to claim the deeper power of coincidence that comes with putting ourselves in rhythm with the natural cycles of what *wants* to happen in this world: schedule at least five minutes of *unscheduled* time every day to ramble with no fixed intention, looking for nothing in particular.

How many times a day do you check the time — on a watch, a clock, a computer, or a cellphone display?

What do you suppose would happen if, on an equal number of occasions, you paused to check *the pattern of the moment?*

You might just take an instant to scan yourself and see what you are feeling and sensing in your body. You might try to listen to your inner sound track. When you turn off the world for an instant, what is playing, what is being spoken, inside your head?

You might take this instant to see what grabs your attention in your physical environment. Even in a very familiar place, you might be surprised by what you notice. Or you might close your eyes and ask yourself what you feel and sense about your situation in a more subtle way.

You can simply choose, in this instant, to be open to whatever the inner and outer worlds give you — birdsong, a phrase, a sense of warmth, a pang of regret, a sloppy dog who loves you no matter what, a news story, the way someone left the toilet seat up, whatever.

Going a little deeper, you can decide to turn down the volume of all the noise and stress around you, then call back to yourself whatever parts of you are not fully present in this moment — the part that's rehashing an old drama, or out on coffee break, or obsessing over the next meeting with the boss, or away with a loved one. Gather as much of your self as you can into this moment.

Now ask, drawing on all the awareness that is with you, "What is the pattern of this moment?" Observe the response that rises, from within you and from the world around you. In this moment, you will likely find that the world within you and the world around you are very closely interwoven.

The Coincidence Card Game

This is one of my favorite games, period. I literally dreamed it up. I have a low boredom threshold, so I am constantly looking for new material for my seminars. One night I asked my dreams to show me a new exercise I could lead in a creativity workshop. I saw myself leading the game explained here.

You can play this game with just one other person, but it works best in a group, best of all in a large group. I have played it with two hundred people, and I have never failed to find that the more, the merrier!

Tools

You need index cards, blank preferred, one (and only one) for each player. Every player needs something to write with.

Write the Answer

You distribute the cards, one per person. You then ask all the players to write down something that comes to them on one side (just one) of their index cards, *legibly*, so that anyone would be able to read it. What do they write? Anything they like! It might be a summary of something that happened on the road, or of a dream from the night, or a quote from a book, or something that just pops up. It can be anything at all, so long as it fits on just one side of the card and is legible.

Make the Deck

Collect the cards as people finish writing them. Keep them face down and shuffle them. This is a card game. You now have a deck, a one-time deck that will never be used again, which is very cool.

Ask the Question

You hold on to the deck while you ask the players to Ask the Question. You suggest to them that in a moment, they are going to have a chance to put their question to the Oracle of the Universe. What is the question they most want to ask? For clarity and simplicity, you suggest to them that they frame the question or theme this way: "I would like guidance on [fill in the blank]." Get them to write down that statement in their journals, or on scrap paper, or simply memorize it.

Deal the Cards

Now offer the deck to the players one by one. Each person draws one card at random. Be sure to tell everyone, as fiercely as possible, that they are not to look at what is written on their cards until they are asked to do so. Since it's almost impossible not to sneak a peak, ask everyone to lay their cards face down, nearby, instead of holding them.

Let the Oracle Speak

Now, ask all the players to pretend that the Oracle of the Universe is about to speak, exclusively to each of them. Whatever is written on the card that each of them has drawn is the answer to their question or theme.

Follow this process: The first player (chosen at random or by the leader) announces his or her theme for guidance to the group. Then — with a drumroll or fanfare if possible — he or she turns over and reads what is written on the oracular card. I've found that the oracular message often needs to be read twice: once to decipher the writing, and again to get closer to the meaning.

Understanding Oracular Speech

What is on the card may at first seem totally mysterious, irrelevant, or ambiguous. Such is the nature of oracular speech. Nevertheless, a profound connection between the question and the answer is almost always found if you probe long and close enough. Other players can now be encouraged to help the person who drew the card, by offering suggestions in a respectful way, as in, "If it were my card, I would think about such and such."

Give this game a spin. You will be amazed, and often hugely entertained, by the results.

| CHAPTER 8 | COINCIDENCE and WHAT WANTS to HAPPEN |

CHAPTER 8

COINCIDENCE and WHAT WANTS to HAPPEN

Most societies have sought ways to understand the hidden logic of events and establish cooperative relations with the powers of the deeper universe.

The Romans grew and maintained a world empire this way. They believed that the divine will could be ascertained through divination, and also that the gods sent signs in the form of coincidence and dreams and unusual natural phenomena. The more dramatic the signs, or "prodigies," the more urgent it became to read the signs right. When lightning struck close, it was certain that the greater trumps were in play, that the game of the gods was spilling over into the realm of humans.

The Romans were especially devoted to getting messages from the flight and the voices of birds. Before making an important decision, top Roman officials, accompanied by members of the council of augurs ("bird-watchers"), would take their stand at a special place on the Capitoline hill and designate a certain quarter of the sky as the place to be watched. They had agreed on ways for interpreting the speed, direction, number, and altitude of birds, and for translating their language.

The most powerful portents, for the Romans as in our lives, were often those that came uninvited. A strange bird settled in a wood and could not be driven away until a defeated emperor, Otho, killed himself. A dying oak tree revived and put out fresh shoots when the first emperor, Augustus, first set foot on the island of Capri.

When signs were obscure and the need was great, the Romans consulted the Sibylline Books, kept — in imperial times — in a vault under the temple of Apollo. In their later form, the Sibylline Books (originally attributed to a great seeress) were a gathering of magical texts from all over the world. The preferred form of consulting them was apparently to spread and shuffle loose pages and then pull one at random — a solemn version of the Coincidence Card Game.

THE DIVINATION DEPARTMENT
OF IMPERIAL JAPAN

In imperial Japan, one-third of the officials in the Ministry of Religious Affairs — the Jingikan — were assigned to one department, the Department of Divination. Their job was to read patterns of coincidence and advise the emperor accordingly. They had many techniques for provoking a sign from the world, including heating a turtle shell and reading the cracks and monitoring nighttime activity in the Shinto and Buddhist shrines where priests and supplicants went to ask for an oracular dream, a *reimu*. But the task of the divination office was also to advise on the meaning of spontaneous signs and coincidences: the fall of a comet, an incident at a bridge, the case of three doves who, strangely, pecked each other to death.

The Japanese word for divination is *ura* or *uranai*, and it means getting in touch with "what is behind." We again have that theme of sneaking a peek behind the curtain of the visible world.

The imperial diviners were drawn exclusively from one family, the Urabe clan. We can assume that in early days this family produced a strong line of seers who were successful at seeing into the world "behind" and at provoking signs and oracles from the other side. They did not need a code to tell them what it meant when the crack in a turtle shell ran a certain way or when birds formed a certain pattern in the sky.

Later, as the diviners became less like wizards and more like civil servants, they followed tedious and elaborate rules. Carmen Blacker, a wonderful scholar of Japanese oracles and shamanism, wisely observes that "these rules, in the form in which they have come down to us, are no more than dead, hardened residues left behind by the passing of the gifted seer." The decline of true seership into hand-me-down "readings" is common in all cultures.

RULING BY THE BOOK OF CHANGES

The story is similar in China, and even more ancient. The Chinese oracle known as the I Ching probably emerged from the workings of the old bone diviners and turtle-shell crackers around three thousand years ago. It is still going strong. In spring 2005, the big bestseller in the largest bookstore in Beijing (according to a sinologist friend) was a new collection of lectures on the I Ching.

Part of the wisdom of the Book of Changes (as "I Ching" is usually translated) is that it teaches us that there is constancy and stability only through change. At every moment, our place in the world is shifting. You can no more stop the changes than ask the waves to stop rolling in. The art is to learn to read the patterns of what *wants* to happen in a given moment. The Book of

Changes reduces the infinite combinations of possibility into a set of sixty-four patterns, or hexagrams — and then multiplies those options by ruling that any or all of the lines in each pattern may be a *changing* line, bringing in further twists and complexities.

The early diviners did not have a book of commentaries and explanations, and they probably paid little or no attention to the numbered sequence of the hexagrams that has been familiar to us since Richard Wilhelm brought the first practical version of the I Ching to the West. They listened to the rustling fall of the yarrow sticks — and probably to drumming — as the binary patterns of broken and unbroken lines emerged. They saw the play of elemental forces and read the will of earth and heaven in those changing lines. The codes pulsed and flashed, bringing directly alive those levels of the mind that are at home behind the curtain and can join the worlds. With offerings and gestures of respect, the Chinese diviners also called on the ancestors — especially past masters of the system — to mingle their minds. The most prized yarrow stalks used in divination were those plucked from the grave site of a previous master of the I Ching.

The early masters of this endlessly fascinating and ever-renewing system for pattern recognition did not segregate it from parallel methods of pattern recognition. This is clear from the story of the great rebellion against the Tyrant of Shang that led to the foundation of the Zhou dynasty.

The cruelty and indulgence of the tyrant and his sexually voracious mistress had alienated most of his subjects. The Duke of Zhou — known to history as King Wu — gathered an army to march on the Shang capital. He came to a river crossing, always an edgy moment for the Chinese, who have reason to fear floods. King Wu was on his boat when a huge and vigorous white fish jumped into the boat with him. King Wu took this as a very evil sign, since a white fish was a symbol of the Shang dynasty, and the one in the boat was big and strong (and got away). So King Wu called off his army's advance.

He spent two years building a bigger army before he led it back, pennants flying, to that same river crossing.

When his troops were gathered on the river bank, King Wu told them he was sure of victory because he had received a favorable response from the Book of Changes, which was *confirmed overnight in a dream.* "It would seem that Heaven by means of me is going to rule the people. My dreams coincide with my divinations; the auspicious omen is double. My attack on Shang must succeed."

King Wu was correct. The Shang capital quickly fell to his forces, the tyrant was beheaded, and the Zhou dynasty was inaugurated.

Let's notice the three oracular movements in this sequence. The king gets a spontaneous warning from a natural event, the leaping fish. Then he asks for a message from the universe by casting the I Ching. Then he gets a confirming message from a night dream. He's letting everything speak to him — the day and the night, the sought and the unsought sign from the deep world and the surface world. We can learn from a man who worked this way to stage a revolution and found an imperial dynasty.

THE GAME BOARD OF THE WORLD

Sometimes we can read the patterns of coincidence and the rhymes in history only with hindsight. Then we become aware of larger forces at play in human affairs, a game beyond our games.

John Lukacs, a brilliant historian of the modern age, has been drawn to study parallelisms in *big* historical events — events that could shatter or remake the world. He studied two examples of this phenomenon from a few fateful months in 1940:

On May 10, 1940, Churchill was called to Buckingham Palace

and became prime minister of Britain, while Hitler, from a command post near the Belgian border, launched the full-scale invasion of Belgium and Holland. On the same day, Hitler sent his armies on a sudden, seemingly unstoppable attack that within two weeks made them masters of the "low countries," poised to invade England and win World War II — while the one man who could persuade Britain's scared elite and his isolated countrymen that "Whatever happens, we'll fight" was placed in the position where he could stop them.

On July 31, Hitler and Roosevelt made vital decisions — without knowledge of each other's plans — that changed the shape of World War II and radically changed the odds on its outcome. Hitler told his generals to prepare in secret for the invasion of Russia. And Roosevelt decided that he would bypass the isolationists in Congress and sell fifty or more "overage" destroyers to Britain, moving the United States to the side of Britain in its fight against Hitler. The conditions were now in place for a two-front war that Germany could not win.

Sometimes it is almost impossible not to sense the presence of an unseen hand. I think of the hand of Winston Churchill, as a young boy, moving model soldiers around the floor of his room, playing out battles and then reversing the outcome or doing something quite different with his miniature men. Then I think of my dreams since early boyhood (when I, too, played out little wars on the floor of my room), in which I find myself inspecting miniature figures in various landscapes. When I look at the figures closely, I see they are alive, and they are no longer just soldiers but men and women and children of all types. In such dreams, I have the choice of acting, as an unseen giant with a hidden hand, to change things way down there, or of shrinking myself to enter a drama and either interact with the players or simply observe them.

In conscious imagination, when I need to understand a situation affecting many people, I sometimes borrow from these dreams and picture myself looking at one of those living panoramas, studying alternate possible movements of the figures involved.

Like coincidence, such dreams feed the imagination. And we may learn from them at every turning. Life invites us to choose between alternate histories — parallel event tracks — in our lives and our worlds. The observer effect comes into play on a human scale, not just in quantum reality. As Rilke says, "Looking *ripens* things."

We'll need no small degree of imagination to grasp what this can mean, and that's where we are going now.

PART 3

ONLY
IMAGINATION

You can't depend on your judgment
when your imagination is out of focus.

— NOTEBOOK OF MARK TWAIN, 1898

The PRACTICE of IMAGINATION

W hen have you said to yourself, "It's only my imagination"? I've said it at a moment of strong intuition — intuition that subsequently proved to be correct — that lacked
supporting evidence in the moment. I've also said it when I've
had a glimpse of a wonderful future — and then betrayed that vision by diverting my energy to listing all the reasons it cannot be.

When we dismiss imagination, we exile the part of ourselves
that knows things that matter in an extraordinary way and has the
power to re-vision and re-create our world.

Imagination is the faculty of mind and soul that thinks and
acts through images, which, as the English poet Samuel Taylor
Coleridge said, are "facts of the mind."

They borrow from our life memories and our sensory experiences, but they are more than copies; they can reshape and transform the raw materials into something new. And they can take on
energy from a deeper source.

The family of a young girl, Sally, who was suffering night

terrors, asked for my help. I gave Sally a toy soldier from my childhood — a Roman centurion — and told her that henceforth this would be her night guardian and would keep terrible things out of her space. I ran into the girl three years later, when she was about ten. "Lex is great," she told me. "Who is Lex?" I inquired. Sally was scandalized that I had completely forgotten the incident. "He's the Roman soldier you gave me!" She stamped her foot. "He's now ten feet tall, and whenever there's anything yucky around at night, he's right on it. I never have nightmares now."

This is an example of how an image borrowed from one level of reality can become a container for energy from several sources. I could simply have given Sally the *idea* of a night guardian, but it seemed appropriate, with a young child, to give her an object that embodied that idea. Through the power of imagination, that object took on a larger and autonomous life. A miniature figure became ten feet tall, and it appeared spontaneously, with the strength to send off psychic intruders. It became a storehouse for protective energy. This was partly the result of wishful thinking (nothing wrong with wishing), but I believe it was also the result of a transpersonal energy — and energy from a realm beyond worldly forms — coming to take up residence in the container that had been made available.

There is nothing *imaginary* (in the sense of unreal) about an image that comes alive in our mind. As the English philosopher H. H. Price put it: "Paradoxical as it may sound there is nothing imaginary about a mental image. It is an actual entity, as real as anything can be." We experience mental images, and "they are no more imaginary than sensations." The confusion comes in because we put down the imagination, wrongly believing that to "imagine" is to entertain false ideas or wander off into empty daydreams.

Since *imaginary* is so often equated with "unreal," we may

save some time and clarity by substituting the adjective *imaginal.*
This has a longish pedigree in the English language; it first appears (according to the OED) in 1647 in this context: "That inward life's the impresse imaginall of Nature's Art." The word *imaginal* has begun to acquire currency in recent times among both scholars and healing practitioners due to the influence of Henry Corbin's work on the realm of images in Sufi and medieval Persian philosophy.

The realm of images is a real world, as well as a creative state of consciousness. It is the region of mind where meaning takes on form and where objects take on meaning. True poets, in all ages, have understood that the realm of imagination is the fundamental ground of knowledge.

LIFE IN VIRTUAL REALITY

Honoring our imaginations is of the most urgent and practical importance because, as the philosopher-emperor Marcus Aurelius said, "A man's life is dyed in the colors of his imagination."

We live by images. They control everything we think and do, from brushing our teeth to making love to speaking or not speaking in an office meeting. Images generate and constitute our experience of reality.

We tell ourselves that reality is out there, but we do not experience that reality directly. "What we experience directly," says physicist David Deutsch, "is a virtual-reality rendering, conveniently generated for us by our unconscious minds from sensory data plus complex inborn and acquired theories (i.e. programs) about how to interpret them.... Every last scrap of our external experience is of virtual reality.... Biologically speaking, the virtual-reality rendering of their environment is the characteristic means by which human beings survive."

Our lives are more or less authentic according to whether we are aware of the role of images and of our own ability to choose and discard or transform the imagery that rules our interactions with everything. Hermann Hesse put this very precisely: "There's no reality except the one contained within us. That's why so many people live an unreal life. They take images outside them for reality and never allow the world within them to assert itself."

THE CRISIS OF IMAGINATION

The greatest crisis in our lives is a crisis of imagination. We get stuck, and we bind ourselves to the wheel of repetition, because we refuse to reimagine our situation. We live with a set of negative or confining images and pronounce them "reality." We do this because we let ourselves get trapped in a particular version of the past or in a consensual hallucination. We do it to cling to the familiar, not daring to give up what we are or have been for what we are meant to become.

The crisis of imagination is pandemic. The 9/11 Commission rightly pronounced that the horror of the worst terrorist attack in American history was "a failure of imagination." With only a few exceptions, those responsible for security could not imagine a terrorist group executing a plan as bold and horrendous as attacking major targets on American soil with hijacked American planes. Yet the plan had been "in the air" for years, and it was certainly dreamed by many people who had no other access to information about it. In the fall of 1998, a New York woman shared with me a terrifying dream she could not understand, in which American planes were attacking targets on American soil, in Washington, DC, and elsewhere.

To address our challenges, we need to draw on extraordinary sources of information and invest our energy and attention in a form of active imagination that dares to re-vision everything.

To be citizens of the world (to quote Marcus Aurelius again) we must cultivate *sympathetic* imagination, which is what allows us to understand the feelings and motivations of people different from us. The ability to imagine one's self in another person's place is vital to healthy social relations and understanding. A sociopath signally lacks this ability.

To bring peace and balance to our world, we require *historical* imagination, by which I mean both the ability to claim what is helpful from the past and the faculty for spotting alternatives to a particular event track— past, present, or future. Winston Churchill was a master of historical imagination, and his ability to navigate through the worst crises of the twentieth century was intimately connected to his ability to imagine the consequences of choosing differently at any turning. When he studied the past — most notably in researching his biography of his ancestor the Duke of Marlborough — he was constantly investigating what might have happened had different choices been made, and drawing the lessons. When he considered the future, he not only demonstrated extraordinary prescience (writing in the 1920s, he forecast weapons "the size of an orange" that could destroy cities), but he seemed always to be tracking *alternate* possible event tracks. As Isaiah Berlin wrote of him in *Winston Churchill in 1940*, "Churchill's dominant category, the single, central organizing principle of his moral and intellectual universe, is a historical imagination so strong, so comprehensive, as to encase the whole of the present and the whole of the future in a framework of a rich and multicolored past."

Of course, Churchill made mistakes. One of them may have been the creation, from the demise of the Ottoman Empire in 1922, of a state called Iraq. But had later Western leaders had the ability to imagine as Churchill did — rather than rushing to darken the consequences of one of that great man's historic errors — we might have avoided the later catastrophe of the Iraq War. Having helped to invent Iraq, Churchill would surely have asked whether it made any sense to try to install a democracy in an artificial country composed of three populations that hate each other's guts.

Whether the issues are in our world or our personal life, the practice of imagination requires claiming a creative relationship with the past. There is an image from Ghana that springs to mind. It shows a strange bird looking over its shoulder. This symbolic bird is called Sankofa, and its role is to remind us to bring from the past what can heal and empower us — and dump the rest.

PRACTICING IMAGINATION

One thing we want to reclaim from the past is the wisdom of the child mind. The practice of imagination begins with making room in our lives for the child who knows it's okay to "make things up" and knows this is *fun*.

When asked why he was the one to develop the theory of relativity, Einstein said: "A normal adult never stops to think about problems of space and time. These are things which he has thought about as a child. But my intellectual development was retarded, as a result of which I began to wonder about space and time only when I grew up."

Mark Twain insisted, "No child should be permitted to grow up without exercise for imagination. It enriches life for him. It makes things wonderful and beautiful."

Whatever age we have reached, we all need a daily workout, and a place to go, in the real world of imagination.

Keep working out, and you'll remember that, as poet Kathleen Raine wrote beautifully, "Imaginative knowledge is immediate knowledge, like a tree, or a rose, or a waterfall or sun or stars."

Build your home in the imagination strong enough, and you may find it is the place of creative birthing we all long for, the state of mind Mozart evoked when he said: "I can see the whole of it in my mind at a single glance. . . . All the inventing and making goes on in me as in a beautiful strong dream."

CHAPTER
10

The SEVEN OPEN SECRETS of IMAGINATION

In one of my retreats in California, I asked the members of the group to come up with songs that had special power for each of them — songs that could give a lift to any day. While some participants came up with old favorites (including the Beatles and the Beach Boys), a woman writer delivered a completely original song, full of juice. It was such fun we were soon all singing along with her:

> Make it up as you go along
> Make it up as you go along
> Make it up
> Make it up
> The way will show the way

There is magic in making things up. The key to that magic is to be found in learning and applying the seven open secrets of imagination:

1. By picturing our blocks, we can move beyond them.
2. The body believes in images.
3. If we can see our destination, we are better than halfway there.
4. The Big Story is hunting us.
5. There is a place of imagination, and it is entirely real.
6. We can grow a vision for someone in need of a vision.
7. The stronger the imagination, the less imaginary the results.

1. BY PICTURING OUR BLOCKS, WE CAN MOVE BEYOND THEM

At my workshops, I often begin by helping people relax and then asking them to pull up an image from any part of their lives — something that happened on the road that day, a dream from childhood, an image that just pops up spontaneously. If nothing comes, I advise people to consider what they are feeling most strongly in their bodies. I ask them to go to that place in their bodies and see what comes to them. There are people who still have a hard time calling up any kind of image. They are blocked.

This is actually a tremendous moment of opportunity, as long as they are willing to give a shape and a name to their blocks.

"I'm sorry. I'm just totally blocked," said the woman I picked to go first in sharing an image at the start of a program I was leading in Rhode Island.

"Tell me what you're feeling."

"Frustration."

"Where do you feel this frustration?"

She indicated her torso.

"Put your hand on that place. Now I want you to follow your feelings into that place. Can you pretend you are moving into that place in your body?"

"Yes."

"There is someone or something there. Do you see it?"

"Yes. It's my father."

"What do you need to do in relation to your father?"

"I have to find out whether I can forgive him."

"What would you need in order to do that?"

"I'd need to get my little girl back."

I took the risk and said, "I think she's right there. Can you see her?"

"Yes."

"Can you welcome her back into your life, and release your father?"

"I'll try."

The next day, in Mystic, Connecticut, the workshop began the same way. Life rhymes. The man I picked to go first said, "Sorry, I got nothing."

"What are you feeling?"

"I'm blocked."

"Where do you feel the block?"

He indicated his heart area.

"Can you describe the block? Does it have a shape?"

"It's big. It feels like a cube."

"Is it like stone, or metal, or maybe wood?"

"It's wood."

I took another risk. "Could it be an alphabet block, like kids play with?"

"That's what it is. It's an alphabet block." Now he was excited.

"Can you picture yourself getting really close to this alphabet block, and handling it? How old are you when you get close to this block?"

"I'm four years old." There was certainty in his voice.

"Can you see yourself, helping your four-year-old self to make a word?"

"Yes. We're making the word D-R-E-A-M."

His eyes were shining. I asked him if there was something he wanted to do to honor this encounter with his four-year-old self.

"Oh, sure," he said. "I'll stop at a store on the way home and buy some alphabet blocks. I have a four-year-old son. I guess he and my own four-year-old are going to have more fun together."

The practice of imagination, on an everyday basis, involves *clearing* unhelpful images that block or misdirect our energies, and *choosing* to focus on positive, mobilizing imagery that gives us courage and confidence.

One of the challenges to clearing the negative images is that frequently we are oblivious to the hold they have over us. Like dust mites or bacteria, they may feed and proliferate far below our conscious perception. They may come swarming through us in a moment of panic, of nausea, of gut-wrenching fear. They often have their origin in past trauma, guilt, or shame. The incidents that gave them a hold over us may be deeply hidden or repressed, locked behind doors we do not want to open.

A paralyzing fear or a numbing block can hardly be called an image at all. Yet there is an image within the fear or the block that is waiting to be discovered, and when that image is brought to consciousness, and reworked, vital healing and forward momentum become possible.

We are talking about clearing our personal history. We don't have a "Clear History" button in the brain like the function you can click on the toolbar of your computer. But we can run a self-scan to bring the hidden saboteurs out of the shadows.

Scanning and clearing can be a simple process, one that can sometimes be done on your own:

- Identify a problem or challenge in your life.
- Pick a quiet place and time, close your eyes, and go to the place in your body where you feel that issue most strongly.
- Now ask for an image of that challenge to become clear to you.
- When you have that image, see whether you can rework it with your conscious intention.

A woman who said she often felt "knotted up" with anxiety did this exercise. The picture that came to her was of a horribly tangled and knotted ball of string. When she visualized herself gently untangling and smoothing the string, she felt a wonderful sense of inner release. The frayed and knotted string became strong rope. Soon she was able to picture herself using the rope to climb a steep slope — a spontaneous image of another, specific challenge in her life — that would have been beyond her resources and abilities before.

In this simple example, we see how the practice of imagination can work in everyday life. First, we bring an issue into focus as a personal image. Next, we interact with that image and try to change it (or strengthen it, if it is positive) with our conscious intention. Along the way, if this is working well, the images will come alive, and things will develop in a spontaneous, unscripted way. That's when we know that imaginal events are becoming real. That's when our bodies — and perhaps the universe — start to believe them. At the end of every act of imagination, we'll be able to judge the results by our feelings and our energy levels.

The blocks we encounter on our roads — whether they are in ourselves, in our circumstances, or both — may be teachers and helpers, as well as part of life's cycles. A block can drive us to discover a new direction, spur us to develop new skills and courage and stamina, or lead us to look again at what really matters in life.

- A block can serve as a *timekeeper*, directing us to pace things out correctly and develop patience.
- A block can be a *test* that requires us to demonstrate or develop the necessary qualities and skills required to pass to a new level.
- A block can be a *detour* that leads us to a better place than the one we were trying to get to.
- A block may be part of a *course correction* that enables us to go *up* instead of just on and to reappraise what we really want to accomplish (and which part of us is doing the wanting).
- A block may prove to be the *thrust-block* that helps us develop the energy to kick off toward bigger things.

We won't know the nature of a block until we are ready to give it a shape and a name — and then discover what happens when we play with it or try to see it differently.

The moment of perception, in itself, can change everything.

2. THE BODY BELIEVES IN IMAGES

An image carries a charge; it sends electrical sparks through your whole body. This shows up when brainwaves are recorded by an electroencephalogram. At the same time, an image sends a stream of chemicals washing through you. Their composition and effect depend on what image you are entertaining. If you are sad and low, dwelling on images of grief and failure, you are manufacturing "downers." If you are thinking angry and aggressive thoughts, you are pumping adrenaline through your body. If you have been able to shift your mind to a relaxing scene — to a cabana by the beach where you are listening to the gentle rhythms of the waves — you are producing a natural tranquilizer whose chemical structure is very similar to Valium. If you can summon up images of triumph, you are mobilizing and multiplying neuropeptides that will boost your immune system.

This is one of the reasons why the body does not seem to distinguish between an imaginal event and a physical event: they both shift the body's electrochemical systems.

So we want to become much more aware of what images we are allowing to work on our bodies, including the ones we haven't noticed.

The power of healing images is now widely recognized in the healthcare community, a very positive development. Practitioners often distinguish several basic types of images that are relevant to health.

Receptive images are those that pop up spontaneously, often in dreams or in-between, floaty states of consciousness. Spontaneous images of this kind may also jump out when a patient is asked to describe what he or she feels in a certain part of the body and says something like, "I feel I've got a choke collar round my neck." Or, "It feels like a dragon's egg is trying to hatch in my belly" — as I once announced to a startled ER nurse when rushed to a hospital in the middle of the night for what proved to be a kidney stone.

Active images, in the same lexicon, are those that are developed or suggested. They may be borrowed from a dream, or from one of those pop-ups, or offered from the healer's own store of scripts and stories. Say you dreamed you went to a church for your wedding, but were horrified by mating spiders who multiplied and grew huge. So what do you want to do about the spiders? Can you visualize bringing in a team of cleaners with brooms big enough to sweep the place clean?

Other types of images recognized in the healthcare community include *process* images, which help a patient to decrease anxiety about a medical procedure by mentally rehearsing for each phase, and *end-state* images, which encourage patients to see themselves in a state of wellness after treatment is finished. *General healing* imagery focuses on a personal symbol or inner ally — perhaps a spiritual figure, or an animal guardian, or a natural force or landscape — that builds inner resources and a sense of confidence.

Imagery used with patients may be "concrete" and "biologically correct" — based on providing a full and clear picture of a set of symptoms and the treatment procedures — or "symbolic." Barbara Dossey, who has played a leading role in winning acceptance for healing imagery in the medical context, offers some very instructive comments on the relative power of these alternative styles. "Symbolic imagery tends to be more powerful than concrete because the creation of symbols more fully engages the patient in the imagery process. And the patient often feels his own symbolism is more meaningful to him or more relevant to his life than a biologically correct image."

Sources of Healing Images

Where do we find the best images to help our bodies get well and stay well?

We can get them from childhood. Go back, in your mind, to a time in your early life when you felt happy and full of wonder, maybe a time when your imagination was all fired up. I think of skinny-dipping in a brown-green waterhole under the gum trees in New South Wales. I think of looking into a crackling fire and seeing knights and castles and valiant quests. I think of dressing up as Robin Hood for a costume party and feeling that I had the magical power to always slip away from the bad guys or take them by surprise. I think of swimming five miles in an Olympic-sized pool on a morning so cold you could see the steam rising from your breath as well as the water — and being cheered by a whole mob of people who knew that I had just come out of the hospital and that this was a big moment of healing and recovery for me.

I can grab any one of those memories and use it as a healing image. You have your own. Once, in a dream, I met a mysterious guide in a smoke-colored robe in what seemed to be an Oriental bazaar. He showed me a Persian rug on the ground and asked me if I recognized the objects on it. I saw they were toys and mementoes from my boyhood — a mounted knight in silver armor, a cardboard periscope for peering around corners, a pair of opera glasses set in mother-of-pearl that had been handed down by a grande dame in the family. My guide told me that if I chose one of these objects — magical because they carried the power and wonder of childhood — it would become a key I could use to open a great corral and claim a magnificent horse who would carry me anywhere I needed to go: to a place of healing or a place of vision. I understood, in the dream, that we can *all* find our way to our own place in the magic market. I have led many people here, in guided imaginal journeys, to claim their own keys to healing from among half-forgotten childhood things.

Our childhood memories may include superheroes or even cartoon characters that we can invoke. The Green Lantern, Batman, Wonder Woman, Prince Valiant, the Lone Ranger, Sir Galahad — pick your character. If that character ever excited your imagination with his or her special abilities, or roused you with the boldness of their quest, that connection still has a charge you can use to tone up your immune system or fight a disease. And you're not too old or jaded to develop a *fresh* connection. In the early days of television, oncologists were intrigued to discover that a White Knight who rode out in detergent commercials was also riding to the rescue, killing off cancer cells in the imaginations — and thereby the bodies — of cancer patients. Then Pac-Man arrived, and soon he was gobbling up cancer cells in thousands of imaginations.

The images that can heal and sustain you may come from any part of your life. Sometimes we need help to find and believe in these images.

Dr. Colette Aboulker-Muscat, a remarkable teacher of imaginal healing whose approach was shaped by her experiences in military hospitals in French Algeria (where she was a resistance leader) during World War II, believed in borrowing imagery from the patient's embodied experience of life. Asked to work with a writer whose neurodegenerative disease had left him paralyzed from the neck down, she encouraged him to picture the hills of Jerusalem — the city, which he loved, had been the source of much of his inspiration. She invited him to imagine that he was rolling over the many hills of the city and feel his spine being massaged and healed. After repeated visualizations, the writer regained some movement and was eventually able to walk again with a cane.

Then there are the dreams. If you want to learn about harvesting healing images from your dreams, read Wanda Burch's brave and beautiful book, *She Who Dreams*.

Wanda had for many years recorded her dreams and had always recognized their importance in all facets of her life. She grew up in a family that believed in dreams, but a terrifying diagnosis of breast cancer — first delivered in a dream visitation by her dead father — brought awareness that dreaming can literally save our lives. After Wanda received medical diagnosis of aggressive breast cancer, a wise surgeon listened to her when she related dreams culled from her journals. Then he told her, "Go home and do something about this before you return for the surgical biopsy." Wanda went home and, exhausted, fell asleep, wondering what he meant.

She awoke with a simple dream in which she saw herself holding a cone breast in her hands. A voice in the dream told her to turn it over, and she saw a vial of dark liquid located near the base of the breast. She took the cone and placed it under a faucet of clear cold running water. The water washed the dark liquid away.

Wanda took the image of the cone breast, closed her eyes, and created a meditation for healing — she saw herself over and over again drawing the dark liquid into one place and washing it away. Days later her physician told her he felt she had literally stopped the rapid progress of the fast-advancing cancer and had possibly even pulled the invading cells back into one place, making the surgical biopsy easier for him.

Subsequent dreams guided her very specifically in mixing a "healing cocktail." While she decided to accept surgery and chemotherapy, her dream images helped her to mobilize her inner healing resources and to speed the work of medical technology while reducing the side effects.

Mind and body conspired to present dream after dream that brought her ever richer and more powerful images for healing and recovery. She developed her own exercises: journaling, taping small messages from the dreams and listening to those tapes in the car, drawing her images, and finding objects to keep their energy fresh in her mind and her senses.

The Gift of Bald Eagle

A San Francisco woman named Stella woke to find that her hair had fallen out on the crown of her head, opening a three-inch bald patch overnight. This was promptly diagnosed as *alopecia areata*

— sudden, unexplained hair loss. Gaining a Latin name was a dubious benefit, since Sheila was told there was no conventional cure. Either the condition clears up "by itself" or the sufferer may lose all head and body hair.

Stella decided to ask for dream guidance. In her dream, she met an ancient Hawaiian woman wearing a star amulet, who instructed her to hold an eight-pointed star ornament above her head as she performed an energy healing.

Stella woke with a wonderful sense of possibility. The next day, she tried to imagine herself back inside the dreamscape, holding the star ornament. She found herself traveling among the stars, with a guide that was no longer a Hawaiian kahuna but a bald eagle. She decided to accept bald eagle as an ally in healing. She noticed that though we call it "bald," this magnificent raptor of course has white feathers on its head.

Day by day, Stella pictured herself traveling with the bald eagle to places of healing and adventure and renewal. And her hair began to grow back. It eventually formed a circle of pure white, five inches in diameter, in the midst of her long chestnut hair. She decided not to color the new hair — at least for a time — to honor the gift of bald eagle.

Harvesting the healing power of a dream image may require us to go back inside the dream and continue on with it. In my workshops, I teach a technique called dream reentry (see pages 86–87) that often leads to resolution and healing.

Swimming to the Day Spa

A woman suffering from fibromyalgia — a condition characterized by chronic pain, stiffness, and fatigue — dreamed that she was at the edge of a beautiful lake. From the far side, a woman was beckoning to her. She was tempted to go across, but she was scared of the distance and not sure whether the crossing could mean death. Later, after learning the dream reentry technique, she willed herself back inside the same dreamscape. She imagined herself getting in the lake and swimming to the far shore, where she found a fabulous day spa with a massage room inside a whimsical grotto. The woman who had beckoned to her proceeded to give her a deeply relaxing and enjoyable massage — after which she noticed that her bodily pain was much less. Now the dreamer imagines herself back inside her day spa as part of her everyday practice, and she has received a series of effective and enjoyable treatments that have not cost her one cent. She has found that imagination works better for her than all the pain medications.

Triggers for Imaginal Healing

Because we are so physically oriented in our society, many of us require physical aids and constructs to trigger the imagination and sustain our belief in its creations.

The Egyptians were masters at making talismans and magical objects designed to give a real charge to an intention — such as the intention to heal or protect. Countless Egyptians carried amulets of the falcon-headed god Horus for protection against diseases or trouble on the road. There is a marvelous cippus (amulet) of Horus in the Metropolitan Museum in New York that shows the god as a handsome young man treading boldly on a crocodile and driving away the spirits of disease.

Also in the Met is an Egyptian water vessel shaped like a hollow ankh (the symbol of life). The ankh is horizontal. Someone drinking from that vessel would be encouraged to believe that they were not only having a refreshing and cleansing drink but were taking in the power of the life force.

In traditional Ethiopian medicine, one way to engage the patient's imagination is to lay texts and images, written on skins or papers, over the body. The patient is encouraged to believe not only in the magical power of such texts to attract spiritual help but in the direct transfer of healing power from the writing through the skin.

We want our contemporary versions of such things. I was inspired — at an exhibition at the Museum of Modern Art in New York in November 2005 — by a fabulous array of tools for imaginal healing invented by Frenchman Matthieu Dehanneau. His tools are designed to help people who require medication to use their imaginations to help the drugs they are given to have the prescribed effect, quickly and without complications. He calls one of these devices the Therapeutic Pen. You use it to write your own Rx with the felt tip on the appropriate part of your body, and as you do that you allow yourself to feel the medication entering your body through the skin.

3. IF WE CAN SEE OUR DESTINATION, WE ARE BETTER THAN HALFWAY THERE

This is the secret of the ancient Polynesian art of navigation, which is beautifully described as waymaking. The master navigator, or waymaker, speaks the language of birds, finds pathways among the stars, and knows the rhythms of wind and water. But above all he is someone who can see the destination. According to Polynesian tradition, this is how the settlers of Hawaii and Easter Island managed to cross thousands of miles of open water without maps or navigational instruments.

The first human to see Easter Island, according to tradition, was a dream traveler. The story is highly instructive. In a time of savage warfare among the Polynesians, a priest called Hau Maka, who was also the royal tattooist, went scouting for a peaceful home for his kin. In a night vision, he flew across the ocean and discovered Rapa Nui, Easter Island. He inspected the location and decided it would make a good home for his people. In the morning, he described what he had seen in vivid detail to his king. The king trusted Hau Maka's dream, and ordered his subjects to gather their belongings and prepare for a long ocean voyage. Hau Maka's people sailed for two months across waters that were utterly unknown — except from his vision — before arriving safely in Anakena Bay, which looked just as he had described it from his dream. The faces of the dream traveler and his king may be among the enigmatic stone monoliths of Easter Island.

As with the Polynesian navigators, our dreams may take us to the most desirable destinations. The art of waymaking now requires us to follow our dream maps, reenter the space and the energy of the places of joy and abundance that they open to us — and get ourselves there in our physical bodies.

Heart Cord to My Dream Love

Marybeth Gurske, a schoolteacher, shared with me the beautiful story of how a dream put her on the trail of the man she regards as the partner of her heart:

"I was single and getting ready to reenter the dating world after healing from a broken relationship. One night I dreamed I was standing in my kitchen doorway, facing a being who appeared to me in human form, though I couldn't make out any identifying features. We opened our arms and embraced each other. I looked down to see my energetic heart pulse with red and purple light. Suddenly, an electric blue cord burst through my heart and connected with the being I was embracing, whose heart responded in kind. We became one and were filled with white light and a feeling of pure love.

"The memory of that feeling stayed with me in the morning, and resurfaced throughout the day. However, I noticed that whenever the love and light entered my heart, it would not enter completely — like it stopped in a certain place. That night after work,

I reentered the dream to clear the energetic block and allow the love and light to fill my heart completely. I set as my intention the mission of finding the person attached to the other end of the heart cord I saw in my original dream. In this dream journey, I held onto the cord and almost swam along following the cord as far as I could go.

"When I returned from the journey, I painted a picture of how my heart looked in my original dream. With each stroke I focused my attention on infusing the painting with the energy of the dream. I imagined myself dragging the cord from my dream and connecting it with the center of my painted heart.

"In waking life, I was introduced to a friend's friend, who was very much like men I had dated in the past. I carried the memory of that dream feeling with me and looked at my painting frequently. I quickly realized that the feeling I experienced with that man was not the feeling I had had in the dream, so I decided to break up with him.

"A few weeks later I met Sam Doctor, and knew instantly that this was the man at the end of the heart cord. As I approached the restaurant where Sam was waiting for me on the evening of our first date, he turned and smiled and opened his arms wide. In that first embrace I knew I had found the partner of my dreams."

Sam and Marybeth were married fourteen months later. When Marybeth Doctor (as she now was) told me their story, she added, "We live very happily with Daffy, our dog, and Ladybug, our cat."

Three Steps to Open the Way

To become Waymakers, in our own lives, we need to take three simple but vitally important steps.

First, we need to turn our minds, and our inner senses, in the direction of our true destination. We cannot do this if we operate only on the level of the little, everyday mind, the conscious ego. We need to reach deeper into ourselves, into our heart and gut, and ask for higher guidance.

Try this now: put your hand on your heart. Listen to your heartbeat for a moment; see how your heart is. Now move your hand to the center of your chest, to your heart center. This is the place of courage — courage is a quality of the heart, and we will only find it here — and the place of our deepest feelings and our personal truth. Ask yourself, *What is my heart's desire?* Let your heart answer. Let images and impressions stream from its core. These may involve finding creative fulfillment or your soulmate, release from illness or restriction, a life of abundance and joy, or remembering and accomplishing your sacred purpose in this life experience. You may find, like Marybeth and the Polynesian Waymaker, that when you find the place of your heart's desire, you will recognize it as a place that has already been opened to you in dreams.

Second, let your deepest yearnings take you into a scene in which you are enjoying the fulfillment of your heart's desires. Be there with all of your senses. Taste it, touch it, smell it — a baby's breath, sunlight on your lover's hair, the pages of a newly printed book you have published, wood smoke on a chilly evening, the roll of the surf. The more vividly you inhabit this scene, the closer you are to manifesting its key elements in your physical life. Grow this scene strong and deep enough, and you will find it has traction. On your darkest days, in the midst of the stress and clutter, this scene will be more than a place to escape; it will help to get you through.

Finally, hold this vision in your mind. Every day, take a break from your pressures and obligations and go back inside that scene. Enjoy it again, add to it, bring in whatever you need that is missing. You are growing the vision of an *attainable* future.

Hold the vision in your mind, and honor it every way you can. Place objects or pictures in your line of sight, at work and at home, to remind you of the vision. Paint your vision, if you are able, like Marybeth. Take at least one physical action every week to keep your body moving in the direction of your heart's desire and to reassure the universe you mean business.

4. THE BIG STORY IS HUNTING US

"I will not just be a tourist in the world of images," proclaimed Anaïs Nin, with magnificent defiance.

We want to be *travelers*, not tourists who are pushed from one package deal and photo opportunity to the next, forever letting others tell us what to see and where to go.

We want to be more than characters in a prepared script. We want to live our own story — not just the daily dramas, but the Big Story, the one that is forever hunting us, even when we have no sense of it whatsoever.

And we want to learn to use the power of story to change things for the better.

"How Does One Learn to Tell Stories Which Please Kings?"

In her beautiful memoir of a harem girlhood in Morocco, Fatima Mernissi gives us a stunning education in the power of story. Her text is one that everyone — in the West and the East — knows something about. It is the collection of tales properly called *A Thousand and One Nights*. As Fatima explains what these stories meant to her, and what they mean for Muslim women in general, we become aware that in the West, we have almost no inkling of what they mean.

Scheherazade, the young bride of a savage ruler who has killed her many predecessors, must spin a captivating tale every night to make the king postpone his plan to have her beheaded at dawn. Her husband is a tyrant possessed by the spirit of revenge. He discovered his first wife in bed with another man — a slave — and killing her was not enough to dissipate his raging hatred and distrust of women. He ordered his vizier to fetch, one by one, every virgin girl in the kingdom. He spent one night with each, then killed her. Now there are only two virgins left: the vizier's own daughter, Scheherazade, and her little sister. Though her father wants her to escape, Scheherazade is willing to do her duty. She has a plan that will change everything.

As Fatima tells it: "She would cure the troubled King's soul simply by talking to him about things that had happened to others. She would take him to faraway lands to observe foreign ways, so he could get closer to the strangeness within himself. She would help him to see his prison, his obsessive hatred of women. Scheherazade was sure that if she could bring the King to see himself, he would want to change and to love more."

Scheherazade keeps the king spellbound through a thousand and one nights, and at the end he is changed. He loses his desire to murder women.

Fatima first heard of Scheherazade from her mother, in the closed world of a harem in Fez. The word *harem* here does not mean a stable of concubines and slave girls, but a closed male-dominated world in which women of all ages are kept under lock and key, forced at every turn to think about the *hudud*, the boundary enforced by religion, law, and custom. When little Fatima learned about Scheherazade, her first and eager question to her mother was: "How does one learn to tell stories which please kings?"

This, of course, is the question we all need to answer, to heal our relationships — within ourselves as well as with others — and our world.

Mernissi notes: "I was amazed to realize that for many Westerners, Scheherazade was considered a lovely but simple-minded entertainer, someone who relates innocuous tales and dresses fabulously. In our part of the world, Scheherazade is perceived as a courageous heroine and is one of our rare female mythological figures. Scheherazade is a strategist and a powerful thinker, who uses her psychological knowledge of human beings to get them to walk faster and leap higher. Like Saladin and Sinbad, she makes us bolder and more sure of ourselves and of our capacity to transform the world and its people."

To save her life, and a man's soul, Scheherazade must create a new story — or at least a fresh episode in an ongoing tale — every night. Eventually this becomes a source of pure joy, and she is no longer improvising out of desperation, but from the pleasure of doing it.

Surely we can recognize ourselves — and our potential for healing and creativity — in her situation.

In the darkest passages of our lives, the power of story can get us through. We may recognize ourselves in the weave of a mythic tale or in something from folklore.

One of my favorite healing stories comes from Japan. It is a story of soul loss and soul recovery, and I have often wrapped its magic around women who are in need of healing from old shame and abuse. The Japanese story reminds us that even a goddess can be wounded, to the point where she loses the brightness of soul.

A Mirror for the Sun Goddess

The sun goddess Amaterasu is shamed and abused by a raging male, her stormy brother Susanowo, who is a hero when it comes to fighting monsters but is no hero in the family home. They have had children together, born magically from gifts they have given each other — three girls from Susanowo's sword and five boys from the jewels of Amaterasu. But Susanowo plays the spoiler, smearing excrement where Amaterasu makes fertile fields and crops, throwing a horse that is sacred to the goddess into the midst of her intimate weaving circle, and so on. The storm god's violence reaches the point where Amaterasu takes refuge in a rock cave. And the light goes from the world.

In her dark cavern the once-radiant goddess sits brooding on the past, sinking deeper and deeper into feelings of guilt and shame. Maybe she starts telling herself that what has happened is somehow her fault, that she failed her consort in some important way, that she failed to give what was needed. In the depths, she has lost her inner light, while the world has lost her radiance.

The myriad gods and goddesses are desperate to call the sun back. They try many ruses to lure Amaterasu out of the dark cave. They call on a wise god, whose name means Keeper of Thoughts, to advise them. He usually keeps his best ideas to himself, but the cold and darkness in the world worry him, too. So he counsels the gods to gather all the roosters that can be relied on to crow at dawn. He tells the gods to hang a mirror with strands of jewels on the branches of a tree at the entrance of Amaterasu's cave. The gods do this, decorating the tree with bright cloth banners, without fully understanding the plan.

The cocks crow, the gods whoop and howl. And the sun goddess stays in her cave.

Now one of her sister goddesses, Uzume, comes up with a plan of her own. Uzume is the goddess of mirth and revelry. She is also called the Great Persuader and the Heavenly Alarming Woman. Now we see why. Uzume overturns a tub near the mouth of the rock cave, strips off her clothes like a professional, and moves into a wild, sexy dance that has the gods laughing and bellowing with delight.

Amaterasu is curious. Why is everyone having so much fun? She approaches the mouth of her cave and demands to know what is going on.

Uzume calls back to her, "We've found you the perfect lover. Come and see."

Suspicious but tempted, Amaterasu peeks around the edge of the boulder she placed at the cave mouth to shut out the world. And she is awed and fascinated to see a figure of radiant beauty looking back at her.

She is drawn, irresistibly, to this beauty, and comes up out of the darkness — to discover that the radiant being is her own beautiful self, reflected in the mirror the gods have hung in a tree near the cave.

Now the god of strength rushes out and holds Amaterasu, gently but firmly, to restrain her from going back into the dark. Another god places a magic rope across the entrance to the cave. Gods of passion and delight lead Amaterasu back into the assembly of the gods, and her light returns to the world.

In this marvelous collective dream, soul recovery and soul healing become possible when we help each other to look in the mirror of the greater Self. Mirrors hang in the temples of Amaterasu today, to remind us to look for the goddess or god in ourself. When we locate the drama of Amaterasu in our own lives, we begin to make a mirror for the radiance of the larger Self that can help to bring us, and those we love, up from the dark places.

Being Caught by Your Bigger Story

It's been said there are only seven basic plot themes in the stories of humankind, but some maintain there are thirty-six, or sixty-two, or only one (with many twists and bends). We've been offered nine personality types in the enneagram, six archetypes in another system, twenty-two major arcana and sixteen face cards in tarot, all of which may or may not mirror stories we live based on our characters. *Ethos anthropoi daimon*, say the Greeks. We translate this as "character is fate," but it means something more, something slippery to our modern understanding but important to wrestle with. It means that character is the personal *daimon* — the demon or angel — that manifests and enforces the events we will live.

I don't know whether there are seven universal stories, or any other number, but I believe this: each of us is called to remember and live our personal and unique story, the story of our soul's purpose. That story may have its origin on another star, or in the depth of ocean, or in the meaty wisdom of earth. It may intersect with other stories — stories remembered in myth and folklore, stories dreamed by those we meet whom we have known somewhere before and with whom (if we are fortunate) we have cause to continue or to heal and resolve.

One such Big Story is the "dream of the forgotten contract": A successful businessman dreams of a night visitor, a man with the qualities of a "simple Christian" who knocks on his door and announces, "I come from my father's house." The visitor stuns the businessman by asking, "What is your contract with God?" The businessman wakes, shaken to his core. He knows, in his heart and his gut, that he must apply himself to remembering, and honoring, a sacred life contract that he has forgotten. He continues to make his way in the world, but he does so with the awareness of obligations to a deeper world, and he does much good in the lives of those around him.

The dream of the forgotten contract is an example of one of the Big Stories taking us by surprise. This particular theme can be tracked through myth, and scripture, and folklore memory. I also call it the "Story of the Forgetful Envoy," and one of my favorite versions is in a Gnostic tale known as "The Pearl." An envoy is sent on an important assignment from a far country. In order to survive and operate in the new environment, he or she must try to fit in with the locals. In the course of doing this, the envoy succumbs to local habits and eventually forgets the

mission. Now a new messenger must be sent, in one form or another, to awaken the forgetful envoy, and this changes everything.

In my own life, with my flawed recollection, I find fourteen
stories around a central theme. I see them in mirrors that become
living scenes, and these mirrors are on the walls of a courtyard
where I find the central character — the theme and identity that
connects all these separate dramas — in a pool of water, at the
center of all. And I know that when I return to this place of mirrors, and remember these fourteen stories, and the heart of them
all, I find new courage and purpose to deal with whatever life
throws at me day by day.

There is immense power to be found in remembering and living our personal mythology, our larger stories. Where do we find
the stories we need to tell and to live?

In dreams, through coincidence — and by making a date,
preferably seven days a week, with the most important book we
will ever possess: our personal journal.

If you are not currently keeping a journal, this is the time to
start. Find a suitable notebook and start writing. Now would be a
good time.

What do you write about?

Whatever comes to you: the color of the sky, the noise of the
garbage truck, the taste in your mouth, the objects you can see
from where you are sitting. Keep writing until you have filled a
page or two. It can be helpful to set yourself a quota until you are
really into this and develop a rhythm. As you continue filling the
blank space, you'll find that two things will happen.

First, you'll find you have lots more to say than you realized,
and that writing like this — without any thought for the consequences — is tremendous *fun*.

Second, you'll discover that while you thought you were just
putting words on a page or a computer screen, you were actually

going on safari. Writing a journal is taking a walk in the bush. The longer you write, the further you get away from safe places and much-traveled roads. You're now in the wild. And you're in that state of alert relaxation that is going to encourage something large and powerful that lives in the wild to leap at you from hiding and claim you. That's how you get your *big* story, the story that wants to be told — and lived — through you. You go where it can catch you.

The moment you are seized by your Big Story will be fabulous. I guarantee it.

5. THERE IS A PLACE OF IMAGINATION, AND IT IS ENTIRELY REAL

A green door in a white wall, with a crimson Virginia creeper trailing about it. You push the door, and find it unlocked. You enter, and find yourself in a garden of surpassing beauty, where a lovely friend takes you by the hand and leads you to a palace where a wise woman in a light purple robe shows you the book of your life, in which the pictures are all living scenes. In the garden behind the wall, you are a "wonder-happy" child. When you are cast back into the world of growing up, and getting through school, and earning a living, and making your way in the world, you are still haunted by the beauty and magic of the world behind the green door. From time to time — usually when you are off your usual path, or totally lost — you come upon that door again. But you have appointments to keep, you're under deadline, you're with companions who would not understand . . . and you pass by the green door, until at last the "keen brightness" goes out of your life, and you lose your appetite for the things you have worked so hard to accomplish.

H. G. Wells evoked this place of true imagination in a wonderful short story simply titled "The Door in the Wall." We can dismiss the story, and the world it vividly brings to life, as the product of childish fantasy, but to do so would be terribly and utterly wrong.

For each of us, there is a place of imagination — maybe many places — that is altogether real.

For me, the door to one of these places is a tunnel that winds through a mountain. On the far side, a path leads through flowering gardens alive with the sounds of water to an amazing building, which combines countless architectural styles without dissonance or confusion, and is guarded by a gatekeeper who asks newcomers, "What is the correct time?" (To which the only correct answer is, "The time is now.") Beyond the gatekeeper is a gallery filled with the art and artifacts of many cultures and times. To touch any of these objects is to be transported to the place from which it derived. Deeper inside the House of Time — that is its name — is a library of which I never tire. Any book in this library opens another world. The librarian appears as a gentle scholar, but sometimes his shadow throws the profile of a long-beaked ibis against the wall. Master teachers appear in this library. I come here often, and have guided others to this place. When we have need — and sufficient courage — we can inspect our personal Book of Life.

If we are very lucky, we may chance upon the door to a place of wonder as we travel the physical world. I know a garden gate, approached through an arcade of rambling roses, in a mellow brick wall behind a country house in Gloucestershire, that opens into dappled greenwoods where beech trees have voices and beings of an order of evolution older and other than humans lead busy and colorful lives. You cannot see them or hear them if the "wonder-happy" child in you has gone missing. I am not sure which is a sadder condition: to have lost the green door, or to open it and find that there is nothing extraordinary on the other side because you have lost the power to imagine.

The realm of true imagination is known in Arabic as the Alam al-Mithal, the "Realm of Images." For the medieval Sufi teacher Ibn 'Arabi, this realm is the "place of apparition" of spiritual beings. It is where higher concepts and sensory data "meet and flower into personal figures prepared for the events of spiritual dramas." It is the place where "divine history" — the hidden order of events — unfolds. While we suppose that what is going on in the physical world around us is all-important, the *real* dramas are being played out here, on a larger stage.

The Alam al-Mithal has cities and schools and palaces. It is a place to meet the masters. A Sufi who studied with Ibn 'Arabi in Konya described his ability to journey into the imaginal realm and meet other great minds:

> Our sheikh Ibn 'Arabi had the power to meet the spirit of any prophet or saint departed from this world, either by making him descend to the level of this world and contemplating him in an apparitional body, similar to the sensible form of his person, or by making him appear in his dreams, or by unbinding himself from his material body to rise to meet the spirit.

This is confirmation from a great tradition of spiritual *experience* of what the "wonder-happy" child inside each of us already knows: there is a place of imagination, and it is altogether *real*.

6. WE CAN GROW A VISION FOR SOMEONE IN NEED OF A VISION

Look around you — at your friends, your workmates, your neighborhood. How many people do you know who are in need of a dream? This might be an image for self-healing, a sense of purpose and confidence, a vision of brighter possibility, even a path to the afterlife.

We have the ability to grow a vision for someone who lacks a vision, and when we do this well enough — so the imagery we offer takes up residence in the beneficiary's mind and inner senses — we can do a world of good. We can work this vision transfer with one person at a time, or with a whole group or community. Great visionary leaders can wrap a whole people in their vision, as Winston Churchill did in the darkest days of World War II (see chapter 12).

How do we embark on performing a vision transfer?

Picture yourself with someone you would like to help. Maybe this is a person who is ill, or depressed, or heartbroken, or has simply given up their *big* dreams, crushed by the accumulated pressure of compromises and disappointments.

If you are going to bring the right vision to another person, you need to understand who they are, where they are, and how they wish to be helped. You are not going to force some ideas of your own on this person. You are going to invite them to be fully present to their own opportunity to be energized, healed, or inspired. You need to start by being fully present to them, which involves *attending*.

To "attend" is to stretch your understanding. You are not only watching and listening to that other person; you are stretching your means of knowing, paying attention to shifts and tingles in your own feelings and energy, and to little "pop-up" impressions that come to you, including memories from your own life. Sometimes, the personal life memories that come to us in the presence of another person are one of our ways of knowing things about them that supposedly we *cannot* know. This is a very practical form of everyday intuition once we learn to recognize that the personal stuff that comes to us in the presence of another person isn't necessarily just about us. This phenomenon is an example of what I like to describe as "What the Bleep Do We Know That We Don't *Know* We Know?"

If I am getting ready to attempt a vision transfer, I need two things from the intended beneficiary: an intention and a picture.

Whether I am working in a formal setting or chatting with a stranger on a plane, I'll seek out their intention by asking, "What would you most like guidance on — or help with — in your life right now?"

Getting a clear response to that can take a while. You may need to help your friend to come up with the right words. They should be clear and simple. "I would like help in healing." "I would like guidance on my life path." "I would like to find creative work that also feeds my family." Those are all good specimens of a clear and simple intention.

Next you ask your friend if there is a picture that comes to mind when he or she is focused on that intention. This could be a life memory, a dream, a scene from a movie, anything at all, so long as it carries some juice. The picture is your portal into that other person's imaginal space. By using it as your point of entry as you embark on your imaginal journey to grow a vision for them, you ensure that you are going into the right territory.

With those two things — an intention and a picture — plus your ability to slip into a state of relaxed awareness and to use your imagination in a good cause, you are ready to do some dream growing for the benefit of another person. Your aim is to come up with a vision that is tailored to their exact needs, carries them forward to a place of healing or empowerment — and is fresh and strong enough to provide traction to move beyond current problems.

Let me give some examples of vision transfer from my own practice.

The Charred Core Becomes Sacred Space

After her hysterectomy, Dawn felt "gutted." She wanted healing on all levels, and her image came right from inside her body. "There's a black hole inside me, a place where I have been burned and nothing will grow."

When I entered this image, I found myself moving into a space in nature that I knew well. I was inside the blackened, hollowed-out core of an immense California redwood that had survived a forest fire. Despite the gutting, the great tree was vigorously *alive*, hurling its green spray toward the sky two hundred feet up. And it had become a sacred space. The fire had created a chamber that was not only large enough for a small circle, but had extraordinary acoustics, bouncing song and speech back and forth across its walls.

I told this vision to Dawn as if her body was the tree. I told her, "You have become sacred space."

I invited her to take any part of the vision that she liked and tell it back to me in her own way, claiming it as her own. When she did this, she rose to her feet, spreading her arms as branches of the tree — and burst into song.

She made the redwood image part of her daily meditation, and soon the vision — in the way of true images — took on spontaneous life. She entered the blackened chamber one day to find it had become the nest of the phoenix, and she saw and felt herself rise, on shining wings, from the ashes of her pain and loss.

Cherry Blossom Time

A couple, Charles and Marie, had separated, and they wanted help in understanding whether there was any hope they would come together again and regrow their relationship, which had once been wonderfully passionate and loving but had foundered on a series of bruising career setbacks and associated fights. I gently sought for an image that had deep meaning for both of them. After sifting and setting aside a number of dreams and life memories, they both settled on a lovely image: of coming together, as if in a wedding bower, under the pink glory of a wild cherry tree in spring bloom.

I let my imagination run. I saw them separated from each other, and the wedding tree, by a wall. They were on opposite sides of a gate. The gate was locked on both sides and could only be opened if Charles and Marie agreed to insert and turn their separate keys at the same time.

This was a clarifying vision, rather than a resolving one. They took from it the clear understanding that if they were to come together again, it must be as fully equal partners — there had been imbalance before — each choosing and acting with independent volition. They also felt that the time for this, if they made that choice, would be when the cherry trees bloomed in the spring.

No Problem Too Tricky

At one of my weekend retreats, a Midwestern man named Joe told me he was not sure what to do next in his life. He might want to retire — or maybe not. He explained he was a maintenance man for a college, with a bunch of skills and a reputation for problem-solving. After some discussion, he decided he wanted guidance on "how I can live the most fulfilling life now." I asked him to give me a personal image. He offered something that popped up in his mind: a coyote den, with three coyotes of varying sizes around the small opening of a rocky knoll.

I let my mind enter this scene. When I imagined myself inside the den, the coyotes altered their shapes and appeared dressed and standing like humans on two legs, though their faces were still canine. The alpha male wore a hat and puffed ferociously on a cigarette. The coarse tobacco fugged the air and caught in my throat. Inside my vision, the smoker's name came to me; he was Coyote Jack. I knew that his bitch — who now looked like trailer-park trash, in a yellow flimsy dress — was Belle, and their shifty, twitchy pup was Beau.

Coyote Jack gave me a business idea for Joe. He produced a business card that read: COYOTE JACK'S FIX-IT SERVICE.

I was skeptical about this flagrant self-promotion by a notoriously tricky character. But the slogan on the card was irresistible: NO PROBLEM TOO TRICKY.

This was rich. I would have laughed harder except that Coyote Jack was now deliberately huffing cigarette smoke down my throat. This was an entirely real experience; I had a brief coughing fit.

Now Coyote Jack outlined the basics of his business plan. Joe should start moonlighting as a freelance all-purpose fix-it man. He could pass out his business card at workshops like mine. He would develop a client base, and when he retired he would be set to launch a self-employed business. I saw Joe happily driving a van with the slogan NO PROBLEM TOO TRICKY and a stand-up coyote on the side. At this point in his possible future, Joe had made fun, interesting friends, and his social life had really picked up. I saw him chatting up a waitress in a diner who was a real fox to him (but no doubt a coyote girl); he would know her because she would press him to try the carrot cake.

When I had taken a long drink of water to cool my throat, I recounted my vision of Coyote Jack and his business plan to Joe, the maintenance guy. Joe became quite excited as he played with the phrase "No Problem Too Tricky" and the manifold possibilities. As the story circulated among the weekend group, several participants wanted to hire Joe for handyman jobs. He seemed to be on his way.

Shakespeare's New Play

Eric Wolff, a gifted and compassionate Manhattan psychotherapist who attended one of my seminars, grew a vision to help Buck, a client and friend who was dying of cancer, to prepare to meet death with courage and grace. Eric sent me an account of how he subsequently sat at his friend's bedside in Memorial Sloane Kettering Cancer Center and asked his permission to tell a dream:

"I sat down next to him on the hospital bed and held his hand in mine as I told him the dream. He had his eyes closed and he listened intently with his head slightly raised.

"Here is the death dream that he used so well:

"Buck is lying on his deathbed surrounded by his closest friends. I am in this circle, and we are sitting around him and doing a reading of a Shakespeare play. While we are doing this, Buck crosses over. When he arrives on the other side a cheering throng greets him. He is ushered into a grand hall, where he dances from one to another reveler until he finally reaches the front of the hall. There are his parents, excited and proud to see him. They sit him in a throne as the guest of honor, facing the gathering. The crowd parts, and there stands William Shakespeare. He removes his hat, bows, and says, 'Buck, I present for your enjoyment my newest play. After the performance I would be honored by your company so that I can hear your opinions of it.'

"The play is performed and afterward Shakespeare and Buck go off arm in arm."

Buck loved this vision, died peacefully soon after — and later appeared in Eric's dreams, surrounded by his new friends.

Vision transfer involves projection, yes indeed. But instead of projecting negative values or expectations onto other people — as we so often do, quite unconsciously — this is about making the conscious choice to project joyful and healing possibilities. It is not an exercise in mind control; we do not try to force-feed a vision to another person. We invite them to take what they can use and to change it around to suit their own style.

Where do we get the material for a vision that can be transferred to someone else? So far as possible, by working with and beyond the person's own images; Eric drew on Buck's love of Shakespeare. We add to that our own dreams and life memories, and the ability of the "wonder-happy child" within us to *make things up* — and let the way show the way.

7. THE STRONGER THE IMAGINATION, THE LESS IMAGINARY THE RESULTS

Imagine that you can reduce pain with your mind, and that you can develop this ability to the point where you can dispense with medications even when undergoing root canal work or oral surgery.

Imagine surgery without a scalpel or knife, and consequently without any loss of blood.

Imagine that you can make yourself incredibly small and travel inside the body and repair its cell structures and balance its flows from within.

Imagine you can travel across time and visit a younger self and provide the counsel and mentorship that younger self needed in a time of ordeal or shame, or when it was on the brink of making a terrible mistake.

Imagine you can travel to a higher level of awareness and communicate with your self on a higher level, getting a wiser perspective on all the issues that may seem intractable from where you have been — and return with a road map that will get you where you need to go.

Imagine a woman president or prime minister in a country that has never previously had one.

Imagine you can travel into the minds and bodies of your ancestors — your biological ancestors and members of your soul family in other places and times — and help them to make wiser choices and draw gifts of power from them for your present life.

Imagine you can go to a place where you can review your soul's contract — the set of lessons and tasks you may have agreed to undertake before you came into your present life experience — so you can now remember and complete your true life mission.

Imagine a workplace that is no longer toxic or constantly stressed out because people make space every morning to share dreams and play coincidence games and check whether an innovative solution or a fun idea has come to someone in the night or during the morning commute.

I have seen all these things accomplished, through the power of imagination.

What we can imagine has a tendency to become real in our bodies and our world. At a Mind, Body, Spirit Festival in Sydney, an imposing Aboriginal healer named Burnham Burnham, his great beard lapping over a blue frock coat, grabbed me as we were leaving the platform together. "You're one of mine, mate, so I'm going to show you something." He drew me to a corner away from the crowd. "Put out your hand." When I complied, he quickly placed two dart-like objects in my palm. "Do you know what these are?"

"These are your bones," I said. Actually, one was a piece of sharpened walrus bone, and the other was fashioned from mulga wood.

The Aboriginal elder's eyes flashed like fire opals. "Then you know they can be used to kill or to heal. That's the nature of power. The more of it that's with us, the more we have to *choose* — every bloody day — how we are going to use it."

Ursula LeGuin goads us to remember that the important thing is that "by offering an imagined but persuasive alternate reality" we can dislodge the mind from "the lazy, timorous habit of thinking that the way we live now is the only way to live."

I choose to imagine that in the midst of our darkness and war, the Peacemaker will come to lead us into an alternate reality of harmony and healing. "Say my name in the bushes, and I will stand here again" was the promise of the Peacemaker to the Onkwehonwe, the Real People, otherwise known as the Iroquois.

The Peacemaker teaches us to overcome evil by cleansing and healing the minds of our enemies, instead of killing them. To accomplish this, we must begin by cleansing and healing our own minds, and claiming the soul's history, and opening to the wisdom of a deeper self.

The name of the Peacemaker has been spoken in the bushes. Can we imagine his coming? Can we imagine it *now*? How can we not? The man is needed here.

"We will change all things if we can make the imagination sacred," Yeats wrote in his visionary novel, *The Speckled Bird*. "But all the images and impulses of the imagination, just in so far as they are shaped and ordered in beauty and in peace, must become sacred. To do this they must be associated deliberately and directly with the history of the soul."

Let's choose now to work with the history of the soul, and to harness the great fire hose of imagination to that, and make sure we have it pointing the right way.

As the poet Tagore reminded us, the stronger the imagination, the less imaginary the results.

BUILDING in the IMAGINATION

C an you find five minutes every day to indulge your happiest daydreams? Can you afford not to?

It is wonderful practice to spend five minutes a day enjoying — and growing — a special place in the imagination. This can be a place of pure relaxation and enjoyment, a place to get away from the noise and clutter of the day. It can become a place of deep healing and creative inspiration. It can be a place to recover your sense of purpose and direction. It can be shared with others. And what you grow strong in this special place is likely to want to manifest in the physical world.

Here's a way to begin that is more than a beginning, since it will give you a place of joy and creation to which you can return, year after year.

BUILDING A DREAM HOME

Picture your dream house. Walk through all of its rooms, study the landscape. Inhabit this place with all of your senses. Imagine yourself enjoying a delicious meal, or making love, or doing creative work, or playing a game, or just relaxing.

Your dream home may be the place you will live in the future. By building it in your imagination, you are bringing that future closer. Be ready for serendipity to help out — for that same house to appear in front of you when you take a "wrong" turn, for the right realtor to just happen to turn up at a friend's party.

If you are really fortunate, your dream home may also be the place where you are now living.

Or it may be a place that cannot exist in the physical world because — like an Escher picture — its structure may violate the laws of Newtonian physics. Maybe it's set in a cleft of the branches of the world tree, or has an elevator that goes straight up to the Moon, or has a dragon in the basement.

Whether your dream house is your future home, your current home, or something else, it is a home for your imagination. Go there frequently. Add any features you want. Explore rooms and levels you may not have realized were there. Be open to changes that will take you by surprise.

Making It Firm

What do you want and who do you want in *your* dream home? Go for it. Don't waste a second telling yourself what is and what is *not* possible at your present age, or with your present money, or given your family situation.

If you can see your destination, you are better than halfway there. Truly.

But I will add a couple of caveats.

Number one: you'll see things, when you visit your dream house, that may not manifest, either because you give up on your vision or because you change your goals.

Remember that any future we can see is a *possible* future. The odds on manifesting any particular future (on eating that fish for lunch, or getting that call from the producer, or anything else in the scene) are constantly shifting.

Number two: dreams require *action*. Growing the vision and holding the vision is absolutely the key. But the universe won't believe our vision unless we take physical action to move decisively in the direction of fulfilling it.

How do we get to the right action?

Step by step.

You have taken the first step. You have exercised your imagination and designed your dream home. If there is anything lacking, go back into that scene and bring in whatever or whoever you need. Give yourself a facelift or a makeover at the same time, if you like.

Now find or construct an object that will help you to hold that vision in your mind. If your dream home is near the ocean, you may want to put a seashell on your desk or your bedside table. If there are flowering trees, you may want to have something near you that depicts a similar landscape or carries its fragrance. You may want to draw or model some part of your dream home.

Next, make a list of the three main reasons why it is difficult or impossible for you to have the things you enjoyed in your vision. There may be a zillion reasons buzzing around your head, but three are quite enough to work on now. Favorite reasons people come up with include:

- I don't have the money.
- I'm too old (or I don't have the looks).
- I can't do what I want because I've got to take care of the kids.

Are you ready for the next step?

Take each of these statements about why you can't have what your heart yearns for and work it over until it becomes a positive affirmation. Ideally, you'll be able to reverse each negative, self-defeating statement — but you may have to work your way up to that. For example, you might go from "I don't have the money" to "I am moving to generate all the money I need," or "I am open to the universe providing all the money I need."

Eventually, I would like to hear you say, "I have all the money I need" or "I am enjoying abundance." And then I'd like to get bolder and come up with a number and a date for full manifestation, such as "I am manifesting a million dollars in personal financial assets, and this will show up in my portfolio on or before October 1 next year." Then — because the universe is listening and *will* respond — I would like you to add a statement like, "I am doing this in an easy and positive way that harms none and will benefit all."

The words you use should suit your own style. They must also resonate with your body and your whole energy field. So listen to your body as you change your negative mantras into positive affirmations. We often fail in our goals because we operate just from the head. The true magic of manifestation lies in growing an authentic vision, through the bold and frequent practice of imagination, and then taking action — including creating the right affirmations — that the body believes.

In the sound of the word as in the Latin root, to affirm something is to make it *firm*. We want to grow a vision, and we want to keep it firm.

BUILDING COMMUNITY VISION

We can "do the vision thing" in a group of any size, and we need to.

For this to work well, create an environment that is sufficiently quiet and relaxed for people to slip outside the box.

Then, give the group a clear statement of intention and an image that can serve as the gateway for an imaginal journey. The gateway image could be a shared symbol, a powerful dream that is relevant to the issue, or a location in either ordinary or non-ordinary reality.

I enjoy using a physical locale that is known to only one or two members of the group. If we agree to travel there at the start of the journey, we can often harvest impressions that can be confirmed (or otherwise) by the person who suggested the rendezvous point. When we discover that we have seen something during the journey that we do not otherwise know about, this provides confirmation that, in a quite literal sense, we have gone somewhere together.

For example, in one group that wanted to grow a community dream of bringing dream education into schools, a dreamer from Virginia suggested her neighborhood elementary school as a gateway point. Many of our group journeyers were able to provide accurate descriptions of details of the school that had not been described — the circular drive, the position of the flagpole, the locker rooms, and so on — as well as a panoply of creative ideas on manifesting the group intention.

After the group journey, one of the participants should take on the role of rapporteur and cobble together a group report. This may be told as a collective dream, weaving together elements from all the journeys into a single memorable story. The process concludes, as always, with an action plan.

In summary:

1. Formulate a group intention.
2. Agree on a gateway for a group journey. This may be a locale in physical reality that is relevant to the group intention.
3. Use heartbeat drumming or meditation music to assist the journey.

4. Choose a member of the group to act as rapporteur. He
    or she will keep notes while group members share jour-
    ney reports.
5. Take time for group sharing.
6. Have the rapporteur weave the individual reports and im-
    pressions into a single report — a group dream.
7. Decide on a group bumper sticker and action plan.

CHAPTER
12

MASTERS of
IMAGINATION

We can grow our practice of imagination by studying with past masters. Here, we'll take lessons with three of the greatest masters of imagination: Leonardo da Vinci, Joan of Arc, and Winston Churchill.

AROUSING THE INVENTIVE MIND
LIKE LEONARDO

He noticed how mountains become bluer the further away they are, asked why, and came up with a theory far ahead of his time. He looked at the crescent moon in the night sky, and wondered why a ghost disk floated above it — and grasped that he was looking at Earthshine, the reflected light from Earth, and described this effect in a way that NASA found quite exact more than five centuries later. In 1502, he designed a single-span bridge like a pressed bow, to span the Golden Horn — the estuary that once divided the European part of Constantinople — but his plan was rejected because everyone else agreed it was impossible to build. In 2001, when technology had caught up with his vision, a bridge that exactly followed his specifications was constructed at Aas in Norway. In May 2006, the Turkish government ordered the construction of his bridge, following his original plans, over the Golden Horn.

Before 1500, and shortly after, he designed prototypes for the helicopter, the tank, the hang glider, scuba diving equipment, a submarine, a calculator, a mobile robot, and something akin to a programmable analog computer. IBM put up the money to build forty working models of his inventions, which are on display at the Chateau of Clos Luce at Amboise, where he spent the last three years of his life as the guest of King Francis I of France. He was also an anatomist, an astronomer, and one of the greatest — if not *the* greatest — painter and sculptor of the Renaissance, an age of titanic artists.

He was, of course, Leonardo da Vinci. The secret of this polymath's immense imagination is of endless fascination. We won't understand him unless we grasp that his power was, quite simply, the practice of *imagination*.

Leonardo has left us clues as to how we can exercise imagination as he did, and these clues are more thrilling — and vastly more practical — than anything you will find in a conspiracy thriller. In his *Treatise on Painting*, he gives us "a way of arousing the mind to various inventions."

The preferred method, he suggests, is to *stare at a blank wall*.

He specifies that the wall must not be literally blank. The ideal wall will have stains and cracks and discolorations. You stare at these until images begin to form in your mind, and then change and quicken. You may see many different landscapes, "graced with mountains, rivers, rocks, trees, plains, great valleys, and hills in many combinations."

Or you can exercise your director's power and let the scenes evolve into battles or great dramas, with "figures darting about, strange-looking faces and costumes, and an endless number of things which you can distill into finely rendered forms."

He does not spell out that the things "you can distill into finely rendered forms" may include a new invention that goes centuries beyond current technology.

Leonardo tells us we can read patterns on a stone as easily as on a wall and get similarly fabulous results.

We can also take a break from visual thinking and see what comes when we devote our fullest attention to another sense: hearing. To switch from visual mode to auditory mode, he advises listening with undivided focus to the sound of bells or the sound of running water. As you let your imagination stream with the sounds, words and music will come to you, and if you let it flow, you will soon be in creative flow yourself, bringing through fresh words and new ideas.

The greatest secret of the *true* Da Vinci Code is hidden in plain view, and audible to anyone — as soon as we adjust our senses.

FINDING A PLACE OF VISION LIKE JOAN OF ARC

She saw things and heard voices. In this way, she received secret intelligence that amazed the greatest political and military leaders of her time. She foresaw the outcome of battles and the death of lords; she knew what was in the secret mind of a king; she saw troop movements and battle lines at a distance and was able to base winning tactical decisions on her remote viewing. Her personal magnetism enabled her to rebuild the will of a broken nation, and she came to embody its spirit. To those who loved her, she was God's chosen; to those who reviled her and burned her at the stake, she was a witch.

The mystery concerning the Maid of Lorraine cannot be unfolded in a few lines. But there is at least one element in her mode of seership that we can all learn from and seek to emulate. In her way of visioning, Joan of Arc is connected to an ancient tradition shared by many, if not all, of our ancestors. It is the way of the tree seer. It involves the understanding that trees may be wiser than humans, and also that doing "the vision thing" may require finding and maintaining a *place* for vision.

In the sculpture gallery of the Met in New York is a magnificent painting of Joan of Arc by the Lorraine artist Jules Bastien-Lepage. In this imagined scene in her family garden, the Maid's wide and beautiful blue eyes reach for something above and beyond the rustic scene around her, though the scene is pulsing with magic. Her left arm is outstretched, and she is clasping something green. Perhaps some leaves from the tree under which she stands. She is leaning against the trunk. She always found strength among trees.

The mottled colors of the bushes and the old stone wall behind the peasant girl in her long brown skirt are embroidery in paint. The subtle weave dissolves the planes and releases a shocking revelation.

You don't see him at first, hovering in midair behind Joan, in golden armor. Even when you notice him, it is easy to miss his female companions. They are translucent, their forms a thin mist through which the background landscape is clearly seen. One of them appears to be carrying her own head. What kind of visitors are these? They are her saints — Catherine and Margaret — and her archangel, Michael, to whom her visions were later attributed. The thing to notice is they are coming to her when she is with a special tree.

The most famous tree associated with Joan of Arc was known as the Lady Tree, L'Arbre aux Dames, a great beech in an oak wood near Domrémy in Lorraine.

The men who were bent on killing her interrogated her about the tree after her capture. It's the third day of her public trial, on February 24, 1431:

> *Question*: What have you to say about a certain tree which is near your village?

> *Joan*: Not far from Domrémy there is a tree they call the Ladies' Tree. Others call it the Fairies' Tree. Nearby, there is a spring where people sick with fever come to drink, as I have heard, and to seek water to restore their health.

Old folk say they have seen fairies at the tree. One of her godmothers has seen them. Joan will not say what she has seen.

The Lady Tree no longer stands. But there is another tree, in the Loire country, associated with Joan of Arc in oral tradition. Through an amazing riff of coincidence, I found myself staying at a chateau near Orleans in the summer of 2005. The grounds of the chateau include a deer park and a *châtaignier* — a sweet chestnut — under whose branches (or *in* whose branches) Joan is said to have spent the night before leading the relief of the city of Orleans, her first and most famous military victory.

The *chatelaine* was delighted to show me the tree, guiding me across rough ground strewn with pine cones and twigs. The old *châtaignier* had survived the lightning. "What do you feel?" asked my hostess. "What do you see?"

I stood with the tree, holding it and leaning my head against its trunk.

Immediately, I received a vision in brilliant, living color, of a knight wearing a white surcoat with the figures of three red lions over his breastplate. An English knight, I was sure. He wore a coronet over his helmet, whose visor was open. A nobleman, then, a duke or an earl. But why was I looking at an *English* knight?

As I continued to look into the scene, other figures appeared. A massing of soldiers around a walled city. I realized that I was looking at the positions of the English besiegers of Orleans as Joan might have seen them, performing a psychic scout before she led the French into battle.

How did she see this way? How exactly did she receive her inspiration?

No sooner had I formed the question in my mind than I sensed a greater-than-human being approaching from above and behind, descending in a beating of wings. I felt its intent driving home, like an arrow or a bee sting, at the nape of the neck. *Le cou*, an inner voice confirmed. I felt no pain, but sensed the pain Joan might have felt, in her visioning — and later learned that before she marched to Orleans, she predicted that she would be wounded by an arrow, as she was indeed, in the field.

At her tree of vision, I sensed a continuity between Joan of Arc and the ancient Gallic female seers who climbed into trees, or into towers constructed from tree limbs, to scout and direct battles for their warriors.

We can learn from Joan of Arc how to grow the power of vision by connecting with a tree and using this as a place to see and to recover our inner compass.

Picture a tree in the natural world that you know and love, a tree that knows you. Go to that tree, if you can, and sit with it.

If you can't go to that tree with your body, go there with your mind and your inner senses. Use all of your senses to remember and taste and smell and touch the tree and the place where the tree stands.

Feel yourself putting down roots into the earth, like the tree. As you breathe in, feel yourself drinking sunfire. Relax into the dream of the heartwood.

When you are sufficiently relaxed, let yourself rise up — or climb up — the tree to a perch in the upper branches. From up here, you can see across great distances, in time as well as space. You can examine whatever issues or situations you need to understand from a higher perspective.

You can take flight from this place of observation, if you choose, and swoop down to take a closer look at whatever it is you need to envision clearly, for yourself or others.

SPREADING A VISION LIKE CHURCHILL

It's June 1940. England stands alone against the Nazi horde that has overrun Western Europe, and Hitler looks invincible. Winston Churchill, prime minister for just one month, speaks to the people and warns them of the stakes. If the British people fail to resist Hitler, the world will be plunged "into the abyss of a new Dark Age made more sinister, and perhaps more protracted, by the lights of perverted science."

But defeatism is everywhere. It has rotted the British establishment, and keeps America on the sidelines. How can Churchill transfer the vision of possible victory against terrible odds? He delivers his most famous sentence: "Let us therefore brace ourselves to our duties and so bear ourselves that, if the British Empire and its Commonwealth last for a thousand years, men will still say, 'This was their finest hour.'"

These words seized the imagination of a people. They transferred moral courage and confidence. Let's notice that two distinctive elements in Churchill's vision transfer helped it to take root in the minds of many.

The first is the *time shift*. He carries his listeners with him into the far future, beyond current dangers into a time where everything has long been resolved. He persuades his audience that victory over Hitler is not only inevitable, but was won long ago — so brilliantly that anything that has followed looks like an anticlimax.

Then there is the *shift to the witness perspective*. He stirs us to do our duty now ("brace *ourselves* to *our* duties"). But at the same time he lifts us, with his words, to a place of eagles. We look down on our struggles from a higher level. The bigger self looks down on the smaller self, and says with admiration, "This was their finest hour."

Churchill brings his audience inside his tremendous imagination, where the war is already won.

We can learn from Churchill how to transfer a vision to someone in need of a vision. Let's review the two key elements.

First, we take ourselves — and then others — through the power of imagination to a future in which an issue or conflict has already been successfully resolved. We build a happy future we can believe in, and that imagined future gives us traction to get beyond current difficulties.

Second, we inspire those for whom we are spreading a vision to rise above the current worries, and look at everything from a bigger perspective. We invite them to inhabit the Big Story, not the old history and the thousand reasons why success is impossible.

We give them a bigger dream, and invite them to live that dream, and bring the world with them.

The INCREDIBLE JOURNEY

This is the first day of your new life.

You are embarked on an incredible journey.

It is a journey to absolute knowledge.

There is no map that will get you there. If you succeed in finding your way, others will make maps of your journey.

There are many false turnings along the way, many roads that lead away from absolute knowledge.

But extraordinary guides will go with you — the guidance of the Three Only Things — and they will tell you when you have strayed from the way, and they will restore your inner compass.

There is no map that will get you there, but you can use some tips from those who have traveled this way before, without getting stuck in the gossipy markets of Hearsay, or the stern temples of Closed Revelation, or on the terrible wheel of Repetition, or in the canebrakes of Half-Remembered Things.

THE WAY WILL SHOW THE WAY

Trust that if you lean toward the universe, the universe will support you. Trust what your heart and your dreams are telling you even when friends and colleagues do not understand and press you not to change.

You'll be reminded that true friends are those who will support you and tolerate you during change — even when they don't understand the nature of the change.

Carry these words with you:

Twenty years from now you will be more disappointed by the things that you didn't do than by the ones you did do. So throw off the bowlines. Sail away from the safe harbor. Catch the trade winds in your sails. Explore. Dream. Discover.

These words are from Mark Twain, a master of the Three Only Things. He came this way before you. One of the things he knew — which may or may not be part of your journey — is that one of the easiest ways of getting to a deeper universe is to imagine yourself becoming incredibly small, so you can enter a world inside a human cell, or slip between the particles of an atom.

HOLD TO YOUR VISION

Tend your vision. Bring it alive in your mind and your senses, as often as possible. Hang out inside it. Play, relax, keep house, create, make love inside it. Do this, especially, on the cusp of sleep, coming or going.

Let the shapes of your vision evolve as you grow wiser and come closer to absolute knowledge.

The house you built in the imagination may change, as you do. It may develop new levels. The people who share it with you may change, because while some soul contracts are forever, some are for only a fixed time and a limited purpose.

Check on the goals you have set yourself, the staging posts along the way. Renew the affirmations you have devised to make them firm, and edit and update those affirmations if required.

Hold your vision in your mind, so you do not become lost.

Take these words from another traveler, William Butler Yeats, who speaks here as magus as well as poet:

> Everything we formulate in the imagination, if we formulate it strongly enough, realizes itself in the circumstances of our life, acting either through our own souls or through the spirits of nature.

Make sure your vision is charged with *desire*.

Don't just park your mind in front of it like a late-night classic movie on your home entertainment system. We get the word *desire* from the Latin *de sider*, meaning "of the stars." Unless your vision is charged with desire, you have lost touch with your star and are bound to go astray.

But if your desire is fully invested in your vision, then you cannot help stirring forces in the world to support you.

PAY ATTENTION

Pay attention, at every turning, to the play of the Three Only Things, and to the contents of your heart, your gut, and your head (preferably in that order).

Who are those broken travelers, flopped, exhausted, by the road, or hanging like bats from the bar, or twittering in coffee shops about how you'll never make it? They are people who forgot one of the laws of the journey.

Energy flows where attention goes. When we allow negative thoughts and feelings to claim our awareness, we divert our energy along corresponding channels. We will then encounter our mind monsters on the road. As within, so without. Whatever we think or feel, the universe says yes.

Take this counsel from Thoreau:

A man who stands in his own way will find the whole world stands in his way.

Don't let others block your way by insisting that you accept their version of what is possible and take on their cargo of disappointment or jealousy. Those whose dreams have been broken often try, wittingly or unwittingly, to smash the dreams of others.

When other people — especially when they are family or close friends — invite you to buy into a view of reality or possibility that is less than generous, withhold your consent.

Check on the personal history you may still be carrying in your energy field. You can defeat your own goals if you are freighted with the burdens of past shame and pain and failure so that your body does not believe you.

The traditional Hawaiian healers known as kahunas have a profound teaching about this. They say that the ordinary mind has very little to do with creative manifestation. The best that can manifest in our lives comes through the creative partnership of the dense energy body (which they call the *unihipilli*) and the Higher Self (or *aumakua*). Get them working and playing together, and the ego will come along.

DON'T GIVE UP

When the world seems to knock us back, when we suffer losses, we need to remember that failing to succeed in a certain situation does not make us a failure. A person is not a failure because he or she fails at this or that. A person is a failure when he or she gives up.

If we give our best to something we truly believe in, and fail to achieve certain results, the project may be assessed as a failure. But that doesn't mean that *we* are failures, especially if we are willing to learn from what went wrong and try again.

Letting go is not giving up.

We may come to the conclusion that, however hard we try, a certain project is not going to succeed. The project may be keeping an elderly person alive, or writing a book, or earning a million bucks in real estate. We take a long clear look at things, and decide to release that cause, to let it go. This is not failure, and it is not giving up.

Winston Churchill was a man who experienced many failures in his long career, and he was often written off as "finished" — yet he survived to lead one of the decisive victories for humanity over barbarism and active evil.

Churchill said, "It is not enough to do our best; we must do what is *necessary*."

So you fell down — even down a whole mountainside, into an abyss. Get up. Climb back up. Do what is *necessary*.

REMEMBER TO PLAY

The journey to absolute knowledge is so serious it can only be approached in a spirit of play.

An earnest man at one of my lectures once asked me to "bottom line it" for him. "What's this all about?" I had the answer right away, and I gave it to him. "Remember to play." And he proceeded to write that down, very carefully. "Excuse me," I said as gently as I could, "I don't think you've got the message."

We give the best of ourselves to our favorite games. These may be games that involve winning or being ranked or being first across a finish line, games in which success comes with prizes and titles. The winnings may include a truckload of money, or an Emmy or a Nobel prize, or survival against adversity, or getting our kids through school — or the prize may be meaningless to anyone who is not sitting on the other side of the table.

The games we play with the aim of winning, philosopher

James Carse reminds us, are *finite* games. We give our *very* best when we are conscious of playing the larger game, which he calls the *infinite* game. Infinite players don't play to win; they play for the sake of playing.

There's nothing wrong with playing to win, or playing for money, as long as we remember that when we do this we are *choosing* a finite game, within the infinite game. The problems arise when we forget that we chose the game. If we are doing something because we believe we *must* do it, if we tell ourselves we have no choice, we are not playing.

Sometimes this happens because we agree to take on one role or another in a game we choose, but end up by losing our identity in playing a certain role. We forget that we *chose* to be an engineer, a mother, a mail carrier, or even a golfer. We spend our days trying to meet our obligations, or lower our handicap, or fatten our bank accounts, because this is what we think we must do. Carse calls this "self-veiling." It is a very serious thing, because it kills the spirit of play.

Though the spirit of play is a characteristic of the child, it can be crushed early on in our children. I think of a very successful businessman who came to one of my California seminars. For all his wealth and status, he was burdened by a profound sense of sadness and futility. "I have to keep busy all the time, winning, winning, winning — or else I'm consumed with the sense that I've done nothing that matters."

We probed the source of his frustration. "I need to create," he decided. "Somewhere along the line the part of me that is the creator got stopped dead."

I helped him to look back over the whole course of his life — to *really* look, in what I call a "goaded" meditation — to try to identify the moment his creative spirit got stuck. He found himself looking into a scene from early childhood. "I'm about four years old. I'm making a fantastic structure with Lego blocks, having a whale of a time. My mother comes in and she says, 'That's great. You'll grow up and make lots of money as an architect or engineer.'" With high emotion, the businessman — who had indeed become an engineer, as well as a CEO — told me, "That's the moment my creative self was crushed. Because it wasn't about play anymore, it was about consequences. I never wanted to play with blocks again."

He agreed that one of the things he would do to release his creative self was to get himself a set of blocks, make space on his desk — and play with them. In doing this, he not only invited his inner child to come out of the shadows; he began to function as an infinite player, who plays for the pure delight of playing.

A similar lesson infuses the luminous movie *The Legend of Bagger Vance*. Based on the novel by Steve Pressfield, it's a parable of how a man finds his "authentic swing" on a 1931 golf course in the midst of the Depression — an analog for the game of life — with the help of a mysterious guide disguised as a black caddie. The player is given the chance of a lifetime, in an exhibition match with the two top golfers in the country, but is headed for humiliation until the caddie helps him to understand that his real opponents are not the heavy hitters but his own self-defeating behaviors and attitudes. He begins to *see the field*. Seeing the field involves knowing such things as which way the grass bends as the sun moves across the sky, or whether a light iron works better than a wood for a drive under a high wind. *Playing* the field is about coming into harmony with everything that is in the field in a given moment. It's about giving our best without fear of consequences, for the love of the play.

The Three Only Things are extraordinary resources for seeing the field, and give us fabulous ways to play it. When someone you meet on the road asks you what this is all about, you could simply say, "It's about playing better games."

ACKNOWLEDGMENTS

The first person I want to thank is Georgia Hughes, the editorial director of New World Library.

The story of what happened when I decided to call her — for the first time ever — to talk about my ideas for this book is a fabulous example of a further rule for living by coincidence: *Notice what's showing through your slip.*

I had just done a radio show on the theme of "The Three Only Things." The show went very well, and I had a strong urge to reach out to someone in publishing immediately and propose a book on this subject. When I picked up the phone, I intended to call a senior editor at a major New York publishing house with whom I had worked before. On a sudden instinct, I looked up the number for an editor with a smaller house on the West Coast.

Up to this point, I had communicated with Georgia Hughes only by letter and email. First contact was made when she approached me for an endorsement of a fine book on Celtic tradition, Frank MacEowen's *The Mist-Filled Path*. Later I emailed Georgia to advocate Wanda Burch's beautiful book *She Who Dreams*. I did recall a dream from many years before in which it seemed that a woman named "Georgia" — who appeared in an American Indian setting but was not herself Native American — was playing a very important and positive role in my publishing life.

I found the number for New World Library. A robot voice guided me through the in-house directory, which eventually revealed Georgia's extension. I punched it in, expecting to get voicemail. After all, she was the editorial director of the house, and such people tend to be very busy and not often — if ever — available to first-time callers.

Georgia answered her own phone and greeted me warmly when I said my name. She spoke to me as if we were old friends, referring to a recent phone conversation.

"Excuse me," I interrupted, puzzled. "We've never spoken on the phone, though we did trade some pleasant emails."

"Of course we've talked on the phone. You told me about your vacation."

"Do you know who this is?"

"Absolutely! You're Robert Moss. You're the author we are publishing."

"That is amazing. I'm calling to discuss a book you may want to publish, but in my reality you haven't even heard about it yet."

There was a short pause on the phone, then Georgia realized she had confused me with another author, Richard Moss.

I refused to hear her apology. "There are Freudian slips and then there are cosmic slips, and I *love* what this slip may be telling us. I'm calling to explore whether you might want to publish a book that involves coincidence — including how we can get guidance from slips and apparent screwups. And you start our conversation by telling me you know *absolutely* who I am and that I am the author you are publishing. What could be cooler than that?"

We had a lively conversation about dreams and coincidence for half an hour, at the end of which time I promised to send Georgia a formal proposal the next day. I stayed up all night to pull it together. The time is always Now. Could *you* resist going with a slip like that?

Countless people — friends, seminar participants, readers of my books, friendly strangers met on planes and in other liminal places — have contributed personal experiences and insights for this book, far more people than I can begin to acknowledge as individuals. So I simply offer my heartfelt thanks to all of you who have shared your lives and your dreams and adventures on the road with me.

I am especially grateful to the members of my advanced circles who have been meeting with me for more than fifteen years in the Northeast — especially in our retreats in the New York Adirondacks — and for several years in the Pacific Northwest, in gatherings where we push the envelope, test-fly new techniques, and play the most wonderful games. Members of my "Dreaming beyond Divination" master class, hosted by Karen Silverstein, helped me to focus some of our methods of navigating by coincidence. Members of "The Practice of Imagination" seminar in the Seattle area helped to deepen our processes for "building a home in the imagination" and opening a space for imaginal healing. Members of my advanced classes in upstate New York, hosted by Carol Davis, and in western Connecticut, hosted by Irene D'Alessio and Donna Katsuranis, have tested and experimented with *everything*, and continue to amaze and delight me with fresh discoveries.

Thank you to all the wonderfully generous volunteer coordinators who have helped bring my work to audiences all over the map, and to the graduates of the School of Active Dreaming who are now bringing our core techniques into environments ranging from inner-city programs for at-risk kids to corporate branding conferences. Thanks to Adelita Chirino and Jim Cookman, who kept after me until I agreed to bring the core techniques of Active Dreaming to the small screen in *The Way of the Dreamer* DVD series. Thanks to Linda Mackenzie, who persuaded me to launch a radio show devoted to dreaming and the Three Only Things. Thanks to Merryn Jose, who introduced me to the mysteries of podcasting and shared her own marvelous experiences of living by intuition. Thanks to all my friends in the International Association for the Study of Dreams, who have kept me alive to the fact that the ways of approaching dreams are almost as diverse as the dreams themselves; and especially to Rita Dwyer, who is at the beating heart of the American dreamwork community; and to Bob Hoss, who, on a beach on the "wild side" of Oahu, shared with me an amazing experience of coincidence that continues to guide my work.

Special thanks to George "Jamie" Jamison, who helped me to get clearer focus on how to bring through the gifts of the Three Only Things for everyone who needs them; to Iain Edgar, for discussion of the role of dreaming in the jihadist movement; to Kym Chaffin, keen student of dreaming in pop culture; to Roni Mecattaf, who was a generous host in France and a key player in the riff of dreams and coincidence that brought me to the Joan of Arc tree; to my fabulous friends Wanda Easter Burch and Elizabeth Dimarco, who have shared many amazing adventures in living the Three Only Things with me, and have helped to grow the work; and to my wife, Marcia, who has generously helped to maintain and protect the creative "cave" into which I am known to vanish for weeks.

NOTES

PART ONE: ONLY A DREAM

p. 23 *"God created the dream to show the way"*: Miriam Lichtheim, *Ancient Egyptian Literature*, vol. III, *The Late Period* (Berkeley: University of California Press, 1980): 211.

CHAPTER 1: DREAMING IS WAKING UP

p. 27 *the root cellar of the English word* dream: Edward C. Ehrensperger, "Dream Words in Old and Middle English," *PMLA* 46, no. 1 (March 1931): 80–89.

CHAPTER 2: THE NINE POWERS OF DREAMING

p. 38 *a dream that saved the life of Octavian*: Suetonius, *The Twelve Caesars*, trans. Robert Graves (Harmondsworth, England: Penguin, 1958): 99.

p. 39 *a young noblewoman named Lucrecia de León*: Richard L. Kagan, *Lucrecia's Dreams: Politics and Prophecy in Sixteenth-century Spain* (Berkeley: University of California Press, 1990). The Spanish text of Lucrecia's dreams is in Maria Zambrano, Edison Simons, and Juan Blazquez, *Sueños y procesos de Lucrecia de León* (Madrid: Editorial Tecnos, 1987).

p. 55 *Wolfgang Pauli (1900–1958) was an extraordinary scientist*: C. A. Meier, ed., *Atom and Archetype: The Pauli/Jung Letters 1932–1958*, trans. David Roscoe (Princeton, NJ: Princeton University Press, 2001).

p. 57 *Johannes Trithemius, a medieval abbot of Sponheim, is now regarded*: Benjamin Woolley, *The Queen's Sorcerer: The Science and Magic of Dr. John Dee, Adviser to Queen Elizabeth I* (New York: Henry Holt, 2001): 76–80.

p. 58 *J. W. Dunne became celebrated in the 1920s for his* An Experiment with Time: J. W. Dunne, *An Experiment with Time*, 3rd ed. (London: Faber and Faber, 1934): 110–112.

p. 59 *Arthur Stilwell was one of the great financiers and railroad barons*: This story is drawn from two books by Arthur Stilwell, *The Light That Never Failed* and *Live and Grow Young*, published by New York Youth Publishing Company in 1921. The Port Arthur, Texas, website is www.portarthur.net.

p. 61 *architect Frank Gehry does something like this in dreams*: Susan Mansfield, "Maggie and Me," *Scotsman*, November 3, 2006.

p. 62 *Dream Music*: "Rock Dreams," *Rolling Stone*, December 9, 2004; Roger Ziegler, "Dreaming Rocks," www.mossdreams.com.

p. 63 *Arnold Steinhardt, the first violinist of the Guarneri String Quartet*: Arnold Steinhardt, *Violin Dreams* (Boston and New York: Houghton Mifflin, 2006).

p. 64 *Egyptian novelist and Nobel laureate Naguib Mahfouz said that a writer*: Obituary of Naguib Mahfouz, *New York Times*, August 30, 2006.

p. 64 *Stephen King recalls that the idea for* Misery *(like the ideas for many of his novels)*: SFX Magazine 45, December 1998.

p. 65 *Robert Louis Stevenson described the central role of dreaming*: Robert Louis Stevenson, "A Chapter on Dreams" in *Across the Plains* (London: Chattus & Windus, 1892).

p. 70 *"Hidden within the grown-up heart," as Rilke sings*: Rainer Maria Rilke, "Imaginary Career" (*Imaginärer Lebensrauf*) in *Uncollected Poems: Bilingual Edition*, trans. Edward Snow (New York: North Point Press, 1996). Stephen Mitchell's translation renders *Atemholen* as "longing," while Edward Snow prefers the more literal "breathing towards," which carries a sense of spiritual reach.

p. 71 *a very illuminating story about this in an Icelandic saga*: The Saga of Olaf Tryggvason, in the fourteenth-century Icelandic *Flateyjarbok*. I am indebted to Valgerður Hjördis Bjarnadóttir, a gifted Icelandic dreamer and scholar who is helping to revive the ancient dreamways, for bringing this wonderful story to my attention, and for the translation on which this summary is based.

p. 78 *the great Persian philosopher and visionary traveler Suhrawardi*: The quote by Shabahuddin Yahya Suhrawardi is in Henry Corbin, *Spiritual Body and Celestial Earth*, trans. Nancy Pearson (Princeton, NJ: Bollingen Press, 1989): 118–19.

p. 79   *In a stirring phrase, Synesius of Cyrene — a fourth-century bishop*: Syne-
         sius, *De insomniis* [Concerning Dreams], in Augustine Fitzgerald, trans.
         and ed., *The Essays and Hymns of Synesius of Cyrene*, vol. 2 (Oxford:
         Oxford University Press, 1930).

CHAPTER 3: EVERYDAY DREAM GAMES

p. 82   *In one Mesopotamian text, the dream guide is described as "one who lies at
         a person's head"*: O. R. Gurney, "The Babylonians and Hittites" in
         Michael Loewe and Carmen Blacker, eds., *Oracles and Divination* (Boul-
         der, CO: Shambhala, 1981): 158.

CHAPTER 4: DREAMS ARE A SECRET ENGINE OF HISTORY

p. 90   *she reported on one of her dreams, and this inspired Churchill's decision to
         give up flying*: Mary Soames, ed., *Winston and Clementine: The Personal
         Letters of the Churchills* (Boston and New York: Houghton Mifflin
         Mariner Books, 2001): 91.

p. 94   *Ibn Sirin, the eighth-century author*: Leah Kinberg, "Interaction between
         this World and the Afterworld in Early Islamic Tradition," *Oriens* 29
         (1986): 296.

p. 94   *traced its origins to the dreams of Osman (1258–1326), the founder of the dy-
         nasty*: Lord Kinross, *The Ottoman Centuries* (New York: Morrow Quill
         Paperbacks, 1977): 23–24.

p. 95   *Mullah Omar called the BBC correspondent in Peshawar to discuss a dream*:
         Iain R. Edgar, "The Dream Will Tell: Militant Muslim Dreaming in the
         Context of Traditional and Contemporary Islamic Dream Theory and
         Practice," *Dreaming* 14, no. 1 (March 2004): 21–29.

p. 96   *Suleiman the Magnificent (1494–1566), sultan of the Ottoman Empire and
         caliph of Islam*: "Registre des songes tenu à la cour ottomane," excerpted
         in Raymond de Becker, *The Understanding of Dreams*, trans. Michael
         Heron (New York: Bell Publishing, 1968): 76–78.

p. 98   *records a conversation between Osama bin Laden and an extremist Saudi
         cleric*: Transcript of a videotape released by U.S. State Department/
         Department of Defense, December 12, 2001. Available online, inter alia, at
         http://www.washingtonpost.com/wp-srv/nation/specials/attacked/
         transcripts/binladentext_121301.html.

p. 98   *according to the movement's own propaganda videos*: These video de-
         scriptions are taken from al-Qaeda videos titled: "Biography of Abu
         Bakr al-Qasimi" and "Biography of Abu Uthman al-Yemeni," Global
         Terror Alert (April 2006), www.globalterroralert.com.

p. 99   *the daily practice of al-Qaeda leaders prior to 9/11 was to share dreams after dawn prayers*: Lawrence Wright, *The Looming Tower: Al-Qaeda and the Road to 9/11* (New York: Knopf, 2006): 356.

p. 101 *Harriet Tubman's story is a remarkable example*: Robert Moss, *Dreaming True* (New York: Pocket Books, 2000): xvii–xxiii.

CHAPTER 5: WHERE MIND AND MATTER MEET

p. 107 *Pauli noted with razor-sharp acuity in his extensive correspondence with Jung*: C. A. Meier, ed., *Atom and Archetype: The Pauli/Jung Letters 1932–1958*, trans. David Roscoe (Princeton, NJ: Princeton University Press, 2001): 36–42.

p. 107 *"We need to build cathedrals to isomorphy"*: Meier, *Atom and Archetype*, 139.

p. 110 *archetypes are not structures but "habitual currents of psychic energy"*: Beverley Zabriskie, introduction to Meier, *Atom and Archetype*, xxxii.

p. 112 *The brilliant analyst and classicist Marie-Louise von Franz, who knew both Jung and Pauli well*: Marie-Louise von Franz, *On Divination and Synchronicity: The Psychology of Meaningful Chance* (Toronto: Inner City Books, 1980): 21.

CHAPTER 6: THE NINE RULES OF COINCIDENCE

p. 114 *Jung had a little garden room on the lake, where he would often receive clients*: Barbara Hannah, *Jung: His Life and Work* (London: Michael Joseph, 1972): 293.

p. 114 *Jung's willingness to trust an unexpected incident — and accept it immediately as guidance for action*: Ferne Jensen, ed., *C. G. Jung, Emma Jung and Toni Wolff: A Collection of Remembrances* (San Francisco: Analytical Psychology Club of San Francisco, 1982): 21.

p. 118 *He gathered his personal experiences and experiments in this area in a most interesting article he titled "Mental Telegraphy"*: Mark Twain, "Mental Telegraphy," in *Tales of Wonder*, ed. David Ketterer (Lincoln: University of Nebraska Press, 2003).

p. 126 *In his remarkable memoir* L'Amour fou *("Mad Love"), the surrealist poet and provocateur André Breton*: André Breton, *Mad Love*, trans. Mary Ann Cawe (Lincoln and London: University of Nebraska Press, 1987): 33–34.

p. 128 *To experience these things fully, Baudelaire reminds us, we need to be in a state of "poetic health"*: Georges Poulet, *Studies in Human Time*, trans. Elliott Coleman (New York: Harper Torchbooks, 1956): 266–67.

p. 130 *The phrase comes from Baudelaire*: Charles Baudelaire, "Correspondances," in *Les fleurs du mal*, trans. by Richard Howard (Boston: David R. Godine, 1982): 193.

p. 133 *There is a forest people in northern Zaire for whom travel is very perilous*: Alden Almquist, "Divination and the Hunt in Pagibeti Ideology," in Philip M. Peek, *African Divination Systems* (Bloomington and Indianapolis: Indiana University Press, 1991): 103.

p. 134 *it was a "mirror for princes," a book of guidance that a medieval Persian philosopher-prince on the border of Persia composed*: Kai Ka'us ibn Iskandar, *A Mirror for Princes (Qabus Nama)*, trans. Reuben Levy (London: Cresset Press, 1951): 28.

p. 137 *Appian of Alexandria was a famous historian in the heyday of the Roman Empire*: "Fragment A: Concerning the Divination of the Arabs" in *The Roman History of Appian of Alexandria*, trans. Horace White (London: Macmillan, 1899): 2:489.

p. 140 *In Fire in the Crucible, his study of creative genius, John Briggs rightly observed*: John Briggs, *Fire in the Crucible: The Alchemy of Creative Genius* (New York: St. Martin's Press, 1988): 278.

p. 145 *Yeats accepted reading assignments from "spirit instructors"*: William Butler Yeats, *A Vision* (London: Macmillan, 1937): 12.

p. 147 *His early novel* Louis Lambert *is a tale of the strange life of a young explorer*: Honoré de Balzac, Louis Lambert, trans. Clara Bell and James Waring. Available online from Project Gutenberg, www.gutenberg.org/etext/1943).

CHAPTER 8: COINCIDENCE AND WHAT WANTS TO HAPPEN

p. 159 *The Romans grew and maintained a world empire this way*: R. M. Ogilvie, *The Romans and Their Gods in the Age of Augustus* (New York and London: W. W. Norton, 1969): 53–69.

p. 161 *Carmen Blacker, a wonderful scholar of Japanese oracles and shamanism, wisely observes*: Carmen Blacker, "Japan," in Michael Loewe and Carmen Blacker, eds., *Oracles and Divination* (Boulder, CO: Shambhala, 1981): 72.

p. 162 *The Duke of Zhou — known to history as King Wu — gathered an army*: James Legge, trans., *Shu Jing*, vol. 3 (Hong Kong: Hong Kong University Press, 1960): 281–84.

p. 163 *John Lukacs, a brilliant historian of the modern age, has been drawn to study parallelisms in* big *historical events*: John Lukacs, *The Duel: The Eighty-Day Struggle between Churchill & Hitler* (New Haven and London: Yale University Press, 2001): 16–52, 195–210.

CHAPTER 9: THE PRACTICE OF IMAGINATION

p. 170 *As the English philosopher H.H. Price puts it: "Paradoxical as it may sound"*: H.H. Price, "Survival and the idea of 'another world,'" in J.R. Smythies, ed., *Brain and Mind* (London: Routledge & Kegan Paul, 1965).

p. 171 *"What we experience directly," says physicist David Deutsch*: David Deutsch, *The Fabric of Reality* (New York: Penguin Books, 1998): 120–21.

p. 173 *One of them may have been the creation, from the demise of the Ottoman Empire in 1922, of a state called Iraq*: At least one of England's prime minister Tony Blair's advisers was well aware of Churchill's "mistake" concerning Iraq. See Christopher Catherwood, *Churchill's Folly: How Winston Churchill Created Modern Iraq* (New York: Carroll & Graf, 2004).

p. 174 *as poet Kathleen Raine wrote beautifully, "Imaginative knowledge is immediate knowledge"*: Kathleen Raine, *W. B. Yeats & the Learning of the Imagination* (Dallas: Dallas Institute Publications, 1999): 23.

CHAPTER 10: THE SEVEN OPEN SECRETS OF IMAGINATION

p. 180 *An image carries a charge; it sends electrical sparks through your whole body*: Jeanne Achterberg, Barbara Dossey, and Leslie Kolkmeier, *Rituals of Healing: Using Imagery for Health and Wellness* (New York: Bantam Books, 1994): 53–54.

p. 182 *Nurse Barbara Dossey, who has played a leading role in winning acceptance for healing imagery in the medical context*: Barbara Dossey, "Using Imagery to Help Your Patient Heal," *American Journal of Nursing* 95, no.6 (June 1995): 42.

p. 184 *Dr. Colette Aboulker-Muscat, a remarkable teacher of imaginal healing*: Catherine Shainberg, *Kabbalah and the Power of Dreaming* (Rochester, VT: Inner Traditions, 1995) is a wonderful evocation of Colette's practice of imagination.

p. 188 *The first human to see Easter Island, according to tradition, was a dream traveler*: Interview with Tuki, who claims descent from the first kings of Rapa Nui, in *Smithsonian*, March 2002.

p. 192 *In her beautiful memoir of a harem girlhood in Morocco, Fatima Mernissi*: Fatima Mernissi, *Dreams of Trespass: Tales of a Harem Girlhood* (Reading, MA: Addison-Wesley, 1995).

p. 194 *The sun goddess Amaterasu is shamed and abused by a raging male*: the story of Amaterasu is based on the ninth-century *Kojiki: Records of Ancient Matters*, trans. Basic Hall Chamberlain (Boston: Tuttle, 2005): section XVI.

p. 201 *A Sufi who studied with Ibn 'Arabi in Konya described his ability*: Henry Corbin, *Creative Imagination in the Sufism of Ibn 'Arabi*, trans. Ralph Mannheim (Princeton, NJ: Bollingen, 1981): 224.

p. 210 *Ursula LeGuin goads us to remember that the important thing*: Ursula K. LeGuin, "A War without End," in *The Wave in the Mind* (Boston: Shambhala, 2004): 218.

CHAPTER 12: MASTERS OF IMAGINATION

p. 218 *a mobile robot, and something akin to a programmable analog computer*: Tom Vanderbilt, "The Real Da Vinci Code," *Wired*, no. 12.11, November 2004, is an entertaining discussion of whether Leonardo developed the prototype for a mobile robot and a computer.

p. 221 *It's the third day of her public trial, on February 24, 1431*: Third Public Examination of Joan of Arc in the Trial of Condemnation at Rouen, February 24, 1431. Transcript available online at www.stjoan-center.com/Trials/sec03.html.

p. 223 *He delivers his most famous sentence: "Let us therefore brace ourselves"*: Speech to the House of Commons, June 18, 1940. Text and audile available online from the Churchill Center, http://www.winstonchurchill.org/i4a/pages/index.cfm?pageid=418.

EPILOGUE: THE INCREDIBLE JOURNEY

p. 227 *Take these words from another traveler, William Butler Yeats, who speaks here as magus as well as poet*: This quote by Yeats is from an address he gave in April 1901 to fellow adepts of the famous British magical order known as the Golden Dawn, entitled "Is the Order of R. R. & A. C. to remain a magical Order?" Text in George Mills Harper, *Yeats's Golden Dawn: The Influence of the Hermetic Order of the Golden Dawn on the Life and Art of W. B. Yeats* (Wellingborough, England: Aquarian Press, 1974): 259–68.

BIBLIOGRAPHY

Achterberg, Jeanne, with Barbara Dossey and Leslie Kolkmeier. *Rituals of Healing: Using Imagery for Health and Wellness*. New York: Bantam Books, 1994.

A. E. [George Russell]. *The Candle of Vision: Inner Worlds of the Imagination*. 1918. Bridport, England: Prism Press, 1990.

Alkon, Paul K. *Winston Churchill's Imagination*. Lewisburg, WV: Bucknell University Press, 2006.

Allen, Marc. *The Type-Z Guide to Success*. Novato, CA: New World Library, 2006.

Balzac, Honoré de. *Louis Lambert*. Translated by Clara Bell and James Waring. Available online from Project Gutenberg.

Baudelaire, Charles. *Les Fleurs du mal*. Translated by Richard Howard. Boston: David R. Godine, 1982.

Becker, Raymond de. *The Understanding of Dreams*. Translated by Michael Heron. New York: Bell, 1968.

Blacker, Carmen. *The Catalpa Bow: A Study of Shamanistic Practices in Japan*. London: Unwin Paperbacks, 1989.

Breton, André. *Mad Love*. Translated by Mary Ann Cawe. Lincoln and London: University of Nebraska Press, 1987.

Briggs, John. *Fire in the Crucible: The Alchemy of Creative Genius*. New York: St. Martin's Press, 1988.

Burch, Wanda Easter. *She Who Dreams: A Journey into Healing through Dream-work*. Novato, CA: New World Library, 2003.

Caillois, Roger, ed. *The Dream Adventure*. New York: Orion, 1963.

Carse, James P. *Breakfast at the Victory: The Mysticism of Ordinary Experience*. New York: Harper Collins, 1995.

———. *Finite and Infinite Games*. New York: Ballantine, 1987.

Chopra, Deepak. *The Seven Spiritual Laws of Success*. Novato, CA: New World Library, 1994.

Churchill, Winston S. *The Dream*. 1947. Delray Beach, FL: Levenger Press, 2005.

———. "If Lee Had Not Won the Battle of Gettysburg." 1930. In *The Great Republic*, edited by Winston S. Churchill. New York: Random House, 1999.

———. *Thoughts and Adventures*. 1932. London: Odhams Press, 1949.

Corbin, Henry. *Creative Imagination in the Sufism of Ibn 'Arabi*. Translated by Ralph Mannheim. Princeton, NJ: Bollingen, 1981.

———. *Spiritual Body and Celestial Earth*. Translated by Nancy Pearson. Princeton, NJ: Bollingen Press, 1989.

Csikszentmihalyi, Mihaly. *Flow: The Psychology of Optimal Experience*. New York: Harper Perennial, 1991.

Deutsch, David. *The Fabric of Reality*. New York: Penguin Books, 1998.

Dossey, Larry. *Reinventing Medicine*. San Francisco: Harper San Francisco, 1999.

Dunne, J. W. *An Experiment with Time*. 3rd ed. London: Faber and Faber, 1934.

Edgar, Iain R. "The Dream Will Tell: Militant Muslim Dreaming in the Context of Traditional and Contemporary Islamic Dream Theory and Practice." *Dreaming* 14, no. 1 (March 2004): 21–29.

Ehrensperger, Edward C. "Dream Words in Old and Middle English." *PMLA* 46, no. 1 (March 1931): 80–89.

Epel, Naomi. *Writers Dreaming*. New York: Carol Southern Books, 1993.

Feinstein, David, and Stanley Krippner. *Personal Mythology*. New York: Jeremy P. Tarcher/Perigee, 1988.

Fitzgerald, Augustine, trans. and ed. *The Essays and Hymns of Synesius of Cyrene*. Oxford: Oxford University Press, 1930.

Franz, Marie-Louise von. *On Divination and Synchronicity*. Toronto: Inner City Books, 1980.

Garfield, Patricia. *Creative Dreaming*. New York: Ballantine, 1974.

Gawain, Shakti. *Creative Visualization*. Novato, CA: New World Library, 1979, 1995.

Ghiselin, Brewster, ed. *The Creative Process*. Berkeley and Los Angeles: University of California Press, 1985.

Grant, Joan. *Winged Pharaoh*. Columbus, OH: Ariel Press, 1986.

Grunebaum, G.E. von, and Roger Caillois, eds. *The Dream and Human Societies*. Berkeley and Los Angeles: University of California Press, 1966.

Hannah, Barbara. *Jung: His Life and Work*. London: Michael Joseph, 1972.

Jung, C. G. *Memories, Dreams, Reflections*. Edited by Aniela Jaffé. New York: Vintage, 1965.

————. *Psychology and Alchemy*. Translated by R. F. C. Hull. Princeton, NJ: Princeton University Press, 1968.

————. *Synchronicity*. Translated by R. F. C. Hull. Princeton, NJ: Bollingen, 1973.

Kagan, Richard L. *Lucrecia's Dreams: Politics and Prophecy in Sixteenth-century Spain*. Berkeley: University of California Press, 1990.

Koestler, Arthur. *The Roots of Coincidence*. New York: Vintage Books, 1973.

Le Goff, Jacques. *The Medieval Imagination*. Translated by Arthur Goldhammer. Chicago and London: University of Chicago Press, 1988.

LeGuin, Ursula K. *The Lathe of Heaven*. New York: Macmillan, 1971.

————. *The Wave in the Mind*. Boston: Shambhala, 2004.

Loewe, Michael, and Carmen Blacker, eds. *Oracles and Divination*. Boulder, CO: Shambhala, 1981.

Lohmann, Roger Ivar, ed. *Dream Travelers: Sleep Experiences and Culture in the Western Pacific*. New York: Palgrave Macmillan, 2003.

Lukacs, John. *The Duel: The Eighty-Day Struggle between Churchill & Hitler*. New Haven and London: Yale University Press, 2001.

Mavromatis, Andreas. *Hypnagogia*. London and New York: Routledge & Kegan Paul, 1987.

McTaggart, Lynne. *The Field*. New York: Harper Collins, 2002.

Meier, C. A., ed. *Atom and Archetype: The Pauli/Jung Letters 1932–1958*. Translated by David Roscoe. Princeton, NJ: Princeton University Press, 2001.

Mernissi, Fatima. *Dreams of Trespass: Tales of a Harem Girlhood*. Reading, MA: Addison Wesley, 1995.

Moore, Thomas. *Care of the Soul*. New York: Harper Collins, 1992.

Moreira, Isabel. *Dreams, Visions and Spiritual Authority in Merovingian Gaul*. Ithaca and London: Cornell University Press, 2000.

Moss, Robert. *Conscious Dreaming*. New York: Three Rivers Press, 1996.

————. *The Dreamer's Book of the Dead*. Rochester, VT: Destiny Books, 2005.

————. *Dreamgates*. New York: Three Rivers Press, 1998.

————. *Dreaming True*. New York: Pocket Books, 2000.

————. *Dreamways of the Iroquois*. Rochester, VT: Destiny Books, 2005.

Ogilvie, R. M. *The Romans and Their Gods in the Age of Augustus*. New York and London: W. W. Norton, 1969.

Panya, Vishvajit. "Forest Smells and Spider Webs: Ritualized Dream Interpretation among Andamanese Islanders." *Dreaming* 14, no. 2–3 (June–September, 2004): 136–50.

Peat, F. David. *Synchronicity: The Bridge between Matter and Mind.* New York: Bantam Books, 1988.

Peek, Philip M. *African Divination Systems.* Bloomington and Indianapolis: Indiana University Press, 1991.

Pernoud, Régine. *Joan of Arc by Herself and Her Witnesses.* Translated by Edward Hyams. Lanham, MD: Scarborough House, 1982.

Poulet, Georges. *The Interior Distance.* Translated by Elliott Coleman. Ann Arbor, MI: Ann Arbor Paperbacks, 1964.

Radin, Dean. *The Conscious Universe.* New York: Harper Edge, 1997.

Raine, Kathleen. *W. B. Yeats & the Learning of the Imagination.* Dallas: Dallas Institute Publications, 1999.

Shainberg, Catherine. *Kabbalah and the Power of Dreaming.* Rochester, VT: Inner Traditions, 2005.

Sher, Barbara, with Annie Gottlieb. *Wishcraft.* New York: Ballantine Books, 1979.

Shlain, Leonard. *Art & Physics: Parallel Visions in Space, Time & Light.* New York: William Morrow, 1991.

Shulman, David, and Guy G. Stroumsa, eds. *Dream Cultures: Explorations in the Comparative History of Dreaming.* New York: Oxford University Press, 1999.

Soames, Mary, ed. *Winston and Clementine: The Personal Letters of the Churchills.* Boston and New York: Houghton Mifflin Mariner Books, 2001.

Spangler, David. *Blessing: The Art and the Practice.* New York: Riverhead Books, 2001.

Spence, Jonathan D. *Emperor of China: Self-Portrait of K'ang-hsi.* New York: Vintage Books, 1975.

Steinhardt, Arnold. *Violin Dreams.* Boston and New York: Houghton Mifflin, 2006.

Stevenson, Robert Louis. *Across the Plains.* London: Chattus & Windus, 1892.

Szpakowska, Kasia Maria. "The Perception of Dreams and Nightmare in Ancient Egypt: Old Kingdom to Third Intermediate Period." PhD diss., University of California at Los Angeles, 2000.

Tedlock, Barbara, ed. *Dreaming: Anthropological and Psychological Interpretations.* Santa Fe, NM: School of American Research Press, 1992.

Tolle, Eckhart. *The Power of Now.* Novato, CA: New World Library, 1999.

Twain, Mark. *Tales of Wonder.* Edited by David Ketterer. Lincoln: University of Nebraska Press, 2003.

Vaughan, Frances E. *Awakening Intuition.* New York: Doubleday Anchor, 1979.

Wells, H. G. *Selected Stories*. New York: Modern Library, 2004.

Whyte, David. *Crossing the Unknown Sea: Work as a Pilgrimage of Identity*. New York: Riverhead Books, 2001.

Wilhelm, Richard. *The I Ching or Book of Changes*. Translated by Cary F. Baynes. Princeton, NJ: Princeton University Press, 1990.

Wolf, Fred Alan. *The Dreaming Universe*. New York: Simon & Schuster, 1994.

Woolley, Benjamin. *The Queen's Conjurer: The Science and Magic of Dr. John Dee, Adviser to Queen Elizabeth I*. New York: Henry Holt, 2001.

Yeats, W. B. *A Vision*. London: Macmillan, 1937.

INDEX

ABOUT the AUTHOR

Robert Moss, the pioneer of Active Dreaming, works with individuals and groups throughout the United States and the world, teaching original techniques to understand and use dreams, coincidence, and imagination to solve problems and reach life goals. He is a bestselling novelist and a former foreign correspondent and professor of ancient history at the Australian National University. His books range from popular thrillers (*Moscow Rules*) and historical fiction (*The Firekeeper*) to trailblazing books on Active Dreaming, including *Conscious Dreaming*, *Dreamgates*, *Dreaming True*, *Dreamways of the Iroquois*, and *The Dreamer's Book of the Dead*. He has recorded the popular Sounds True audio series *Dream Gates: A Journey into Active Dreaming*. He lives in upstate New York.

FOR MORE INFORMATION

Robert Moss gives lectures, seminars, and workshops all over the world, and he leads a School of Active Dreaming that offers a three-year training for teachers of his techniques. He has produced an educational DVD series, *The Way of the Dreamer*, and a drumming CD to facilitate dream reentry and conscious visioning. Both are available from:

Psyche Productions
23 Crown Street
Milford, CT 06460
(203) 877-9315
www.psycheproductions.net

He hosts a radio show devoted to the Three Only Things. To contact Robert, and for complete information on all his programs and other publications, please visit his website:

www.mossdreams.com